LAUNCHCODE:

Pharma, AI and The Next Frontier

Volume 1: The Agentic Shift

Larry Mickelberg

To every patient I met behind the pharmacy counter in Philadelphia, who reminded me that healthcare begins with trust, understanding, and human connection.

And to those working tirelessly across the life sciences industry— may we never lose sight of the people behind the data, even as we build the future with code, algorithms, and AI.

This book is for those who believe that technology should serve humanity, and that the soul of healthcare is not just in science, but in empathy.

Acknowledgements

This book is the culmination of decades of work across the healthcare and marketing industries — and I owe a deep debt of gratitude to the people who've shaped that journey.

To my wife, **Jessica,** thank you for your patience, encouragement, and steady belief in me. Your love and support make the long hours and late nights worth it.

To the many colleagues, mentors, clients, and collaborators I've been fortunate to learn from — across **Medical Broadcasting Company, Digitas Health, Havas Health, Deloitte, Publicis Health**, and now AXONAL.AI — thank you for challenging my thinking, sharpening my vision, and reminding me that real progress is built on shared insight and relentless curiosity.

I'd also like to acknowledge the role of **artificial intelligence** in the creation of this book. From organizing early drafts to refining ideas and exploring new perspectives, AI was not just a subject of the book — it was part of the process. This collaboration between human thought and machine assistance reflects the very theme at the heart of this work: when guided with purpose, technology can enhance clarity, creativity, and impact.

Finally, to the broader healthcare community — the scientists, strategists, marketers, technologists, and changemakers — thank you for continuing to push boundaries in service of better outcomes. This book is for you.

Contents

Introduction

Before We Begin

I didn't write this book because I had a grand theory to share. I wrote it because I kept seeing the same frustrating pattern. Strong science. Smart teams. Serious budgets. And still, something between approval and adoption would break down. Maybe the field force didn't have the right context. Maybe the messaging missed the moment. Maybe a patient never made it past step one. Not because people weren't trying. But because the system wasn't built for the complexity we're now facing. Over time, I stopped asking, "How do we fix this part?" And started asking:

What if the entire model needs to change?

Why This Book?

This isn't about layering new tools on top of old habits. It's about stepping back and reimagining how commercialization can actually work. It's about recognizing that speed, precision, and learning aren't buzzwords anymore. They're the baseline. And the only way to meet that bar is by re-architecting the system itself. That's what this book explores.

What You'll Find

This first volume lays out the case for a new commercial operating model—one powered by intelligent agents and designed to orchestrate, not just execute.

You'll meet the concept of **Launchcode,** our name for this AI-native architecture—and see how each piece fits into a commercial system that adapts in real-time.

Yes, there's some jargon. But underneath it all is a simple idea: We can build something better.

A Personal Note

I've spent over two decades in healthcare commercialization. I've seen incredible moments and launches that changed lives. But I've also seen waste, friction, and missed opportunities that shouldn't have happened. This book is for anyone who's ever looked at the system and thought: *there has to be a better way.*

I believe there is.

Let's build it together.

—Larry

Chapter 1: The AI Commercial Era Begins

A New Morning

It's 2035, and the system feels... different.

Sales meetings aren't just shorter—they're sharper. Messaging hits home, tuned to each provider's priorities. Launches aren't chaotic—they're calm and coordinated. Payer conversations feel less combative. Patient access is quicker. And the support? Finally personal. Finally timely. It didn't happen in one big leap. It happened quietly, behind the scenes, one intelligent action at a time. This is the AI Commercial Era—a world where science still leads, but commercialization finally keeps pace.

And it didn't start with a single breakthrough. It started with a question: **What if the commercial system could learn?**

Rewinding the Playbook

For decades, the industry ran on a familiar cadence. If you built a solid brand plan, trained your reps, and launched a good campaign, the market would reward you.

That rhythm served us well—especially in the era of blockbuster drugs. Mass reach worked. Reps had access. Providers were receptive. Brand cycles moved slowly. And success was often a matter of scale: more reps, more reach, more scripts. It was a reliable engine until it wasn't. By the mid-2000s, the engine started sputtering. Electronic medical records shifted how doctors consumed information. Digital tools appeared—but weren't connected. HCP access declined, especially in systems and cities.

Patients expected the same personalized experiences they got from consumer brands. Payers changed the rules—frequently, regionally, and without warning.

But instead of rethinking the machine, we kept bolting on fixes. Omnichannel, but with the same annual brand plan. Dashboards, but still top-down decision-making. Digital campaigns, but disconnected from reps. We modernized the surface. But the core? They are still running a playbook from another era.

Legacy Feature	Modern Limitation
Annual brand plans	Obsolete by Q2, unable to adapt in real-time
Static message grids	Misaligned with HCP expectations and signal
Manual rep planning	Blind to digital behavior, payer changes, and access realities
Siloed execution	Fragmented HCP and patient experiences
Lagging KPIs	Insights came too late to influence action.

When Complexity Outpaced Control

By the early 2020s, we were asking our systems to do too much—and getting too little in return.

Here's where things broke down:

We had data. We had dashboards. But the system wasn't built to respond. It was like running a smart car on a paper map.

Why Digital Alone Wasn't the Answer

Let's be honest: pharma invested heavily in digital. But transformation doesn't happen by adding tools. It happens by rethinking the system they're meant to support.

Too often, "digital" meant:

- Pushing more content.

- Building more dashboards.

- Automating emails.

- Managing compliance workflows.

But none of that tackled the real issue: our system was still **manual, rigid, and reactive**.

We were digitizing inefficiency. A campaign ends. A rep gets results. But doesn't know what to do with them. A payer shifts coverage. Field teams find out **weeks** later. A patient stops therapy. And the system shrugs—because no one's tuned to catch the signal.

And the Human Cost?

It was real. Brand teams sat in meetings... about meetings. Reps second-guessed every call. Managers coached off outdated reports. Marketers made more content, not better journeys. Compliance turned into a traffic jam instead of a guide rail. Everyone was working harder. But the results didn't budge because hard work can't solve a structural problem.

When the System Couldn't Keep Up with Science

Eventually, leadership noticed the same pattern everywhere:

- More launches missing first-year targets.

- Diminishing ROI on field investments.

- Budgets harder to defend.

- Increasing complexity—and slower reactions.

- Patient outcomes falling behind therapeutic advances.

And the biggest red flag?

Commercial speed couldn't keep up with scientific innovation.

You don't spend a billion dollars developing a breakthrough therapy just to watch commercialization slow it down. The cost wasn't just operational. It was strategic.

A Familiar Pattern

And it wasn't limited to one company or one team.

The same symptoms showed up across the industry:

- Oncology brands stalled post-launch due to invisible coverage issues.
- Neurology reps chased disengaged HCPs.
- Rare disease launches got delayed due to onboarding bottlenecks.
- Immunology brands spent big on content... that no one read.
- Primary care teams pushed TRx without insight into refill behavior.

The common thread?

The commercial system was too slow, too disconnected, and too brittle.

The Quiet Turning Point

Around 2023, the questions started shifting.

Instead of, "How can we optimize what we have?" leaders started asking:

- What if our system could learn?

- What if reps and digital worked as one?

- What if we saw friction coming—before it happened?

- What if our brand plans were living frameworks, not rigid scripts?

These weren't just tech questions. They were design questions. Because it had become clear, that we didn't need more dashboards.

We needed a new system.

The Rise of the Intelligent System

Back to that morning in 2035.

Dr. Simone Carter walks into her office, latte in hand, tablet already in sync. No calls. No emails. No last-minute fire drills. But she knows exactly what matters.

A new migraine treatment just became preferred on a key payer formulary. One of her patients—flagged as a likely responder—has already filled a 90-day prescription. Coverage is confirmed. Co-pay applied. Onboarding in motion.

She glances at the concise, personalized summary and smiles. It's clinical. It's clear. And it took her 30 seconds. She hasn't been pitched. She hasn't been pressured.

But somehow, the right thing happened at the right time. Because behind that experience is something new: an intelligent commercial system. One that doesn't wait for people to coordinate. One that sees, decides, and acts—without asking Dr. Carter to carry the burden.

This is orchestration—not magic.

From Static to Systemic

Legacy commercialization was built on campaigns.

Teams created brand plans, executed by channel, and tracked performance after the fact. The assumption was simple: if every team did their job—field, access, digital, support—the sum would be a success.

But the market broke that assumption.

Great messaging fails if it's out of sync with the payer policy.

Field teams fall short if patients hit onboarding walls. Support programs don't help if the patient never gets past step one. You can't fix a fragmented system by working harder. You need something that works **smarter**. You need a commercial system that's always listening, always learning, always moving.

Enter Launchcode

We call that system **Launchcode**.

Launchcode isn't a tool or, a vendor or a platform.

It's a modular, intelligent operating model—powered by a network of AI agents, each responsible for a critical part of the commercial journey. Together, they form a closed-loop system designed to adapt in real-time.

Let's break it down:

Agent	Function
Targeting Agent	Detects engagement patterns, adjusts HCP prioritization dynamically
Messaging Agent	Selects, sequences, and tests content variants across every channel
Access Agent	Models payer behavior, forecasts friction, and adapts access strategy
Field Agent	Orchestrates rep activity with signal-based precision and timing
Patient Agent	Personalizes onboarding and support using behavioral and coverage data
Performance Agent	Measures what works, attributes results, and feeds system-wide learning

Each agent operates independently, but together, they do something game-changing:

They **replace the brand plan** with real-time orchestration.

Not Just Automation. Orchestration.

Here's where we draw the line.

Launchcode is not automated.

Automation reduces human effort. Launchcode **increases commercial precision**.

Automation sends the same message faster. Launchcode sends the **right** message to the **right** person through the **right** channel—based on the actual market signal.

Imagine it like air traffic control:

- **Targeting** is radar—scanning the sky for best paths.
- **Messaging** is the pilot comms—ensuring timing and clarity.
- **Access** is the weather system—anticipating turbulence.
- **The field** is flight ops—sequencing takeoffs and landings.
- **The patient** gets everyone to their gate.

- **Performance** watches it all—re-routing when needed.

It's not about flying faster. It's about flying **smarter**.

A Launch: MigraRelief

Let's bring this to life.

In 2033, a mid-sized neurology brand, **MigraRelief**, prepared for launch.

In the old world, they would've followed a familiar cycle:

- Finalize a 12-month plan.
- Use decile lists for HCP targeting.
- Lock 6 messages in MLR.
- Deploy the field force nationally.
- Add digital and patient support post-launch.

Instead, they turned on Launchcode.

Here's what happened:

- **Targeting Agent** used EMR + referral data to identify high-potential HCPs.
- **Messaging Agent** tested 30 variants in pre-launch simulations, selecting the top 3 per segment.
- **Access Agent** modelled 20 payer regions and flagged 3 high-risk zones.
- **Field Agent** sequenced rep visits based on signal, policy, and behavior.
- **Patient Agent** launched 1:1 onboarding within 12 hours of the first Rx.

- **Performance Agent** monitored all patterns, feeding improvement loops.

Results within 60 days:

Metric	Outcome
Time to therapy	18% faster
High-priority HCP conversion	22% higher
Refill abandonment	28% lower
TRx forecast lift (early geos)	15% above plan

Same product. Same science.

Different system.

What About the Team?

Here's a common misconception: that systems like Launchcode replace teams. Not even close.

They **amplify** what teams do best.

- **Brand leads** stop managing PowerPoints—they architect systems.

- **Field managers** don't just motivate—they coach in real-time.

- **Marketers** stop chasing channel volume—they define experiment frameworks.

- **Compliance** becomes a boundary-setter, not a bottleneck.

This isn't downsizing. It's reallocation—to where humans thrive.

Built for Compliance

Let's talk regulation.

Launchcode was designed for regulated environments from day one.

- Content is modular and versioned.

- Logic is rules-based.

- Every action is logged, traceable, and auditable.

- Deviations escalate, not disappear.

Compliance teams don't lose control. They **design the rules the system plays by**.

Want to limit message variants by channel? You can. Need thresholds for patient contact? Already built in. This isn't AI running loose. This is AI that respects boundaries—because they're embedded from the start.

What It Means for Patients

Remember Dr. Carter's patient—Joanna, age 45, newly diagnosed with chronic migraines?

Before Launchcode:

- Rx sent to the pharmacy.

- Prior auth flagged—delays start.

- The support program waits two weeks.

- Joanna never starts therapy.

With Launchcode:

- **Access Agent** predicts the PA barrier **before** the Rx is written.

- **Patient Agent** launches onboarding the same day.

- **Co-pay enrollment** was completed in minutes.
- Therapy begins within 72 hours.

It's not a chatbot. It's a system that *cares enough to coordinate.*

A Leadership Call to Action

So, if you're a commercial leader, ask yourself:

- Are we planning around quarters while the market moves weekly?
- Are our reps working off static lists—or dynamic signals?
- Are we optimizing campaigns—or orchestrating outcomes?

Launchcode doesn't ask you to buy a tool. It asks you to lead with a **new model**.

Traditional Role	New Role
Brand Manager	Commercial System Architect
Field Rep	Orchestrated Engagement Specialist
Digital Marketer	Messaging Framework Optimizer
MLR Reviewer	Governance Rules Designer
Insights Analyst	Signal Interpreter and Agent Tuner

A model where:

- Strategy is encoded in systems.
- Teams work with agents, not dashboards.
- Data doesn't just inform—it drives action.
- Patients don't wait for the system to catch up.

This isn't a pitch.

It's already in motion.

The question is: **Are you building for the world that's coming—or the one that's passing?**

What's Next

In the chapters ahead, we'll break down each agent, explore how to deploy and govern them and show how to redesign your commercial organization for this new era. But first, it starts here—with one simple truth:

We need a better system.

Because the one we inherited was built for a different time.

And the one we need? It's already running.

Let's build it—together.

A Personal Note

I've worked in healthcare commercialization for more than two decades. I've seen the system do incredible things—connecting breakthroughs to people who need them most. But I've also seen waste. Complexity. Misalignment. And missed opportunities to help patients sooner, more clearly, and more equitably.

I wrote this book not just to outline what's possible—but to challenge us to build **what comes next**. Because we're not just optimizing for better campaigns. We're reimagining how the entire commercial engine works. The future won't be built by those who resist change. It will be led by those who **orchestrate it.**

Let's begin.

Chapter 2: The Case for Change

When the System Can't Keep Up

It wasn't a single event that signalled the system was breaking. It was a series of subtle but undeniable shifts—boardroom frustrations, missed forecasts, rising field tension, digital fatigue, payer pushback, and, above all, patients who waited longer than they should have.

The cracks in the old commercial model aren't theoretical. They're measurable. And they're widening under pressure. Across the industry, brand leaders are being asked to do more, faster, with fewer resources—and to deliver not just activity but outcomes. All while operating in a market that changes faster than traditional playbooks can handle.

Welcome to the pressure cooker of modern pharmaceutical commercialization.

The Everyday Strain of the Old Model

You don't need a dashboard to know something's wrong.

You see it in launch retrospectives. You hear it in field manager meetings. You feel it when a product with world-class science struggles to reach the patients who need it.

Ask any commercial leader, and the symptoms will sound familiar:

- Budgets are flattening—even as expectations rise.
- Payer dynamics are shifting mid-cycle.

- Content volumes are increasing, but engagement is declining.

- Field effectiveness is harder to measure—and harder to prove.

- Brand teams are moving faster but struggling to keep up.

The stakes are real: if we don't commercialize better, innovation won't translate into impact. And right now, the gap between the two is growing wider by the quarter.

A Familiar Failure

Take a specialty product launch—an experience that echoes across dozens of companies each year.

The science is strong. The unmet need is clear. The forecast is ambitious.

But within six months, reality starts to bite:

- Access is tighter than modeled: step edits, prior auths, and regional delays.

- HCP access declines: reps face more no-see offices or get replaced by digital.

- Messaging misses: value isn't translating into prescribing behavior.

- Content saturation sets in: open rates drop, personalization lags.

- Patient support is too slow: drop-off happens before onboarding even begins.

It's not about bad execution. It's about misaligned execution.

The team worked hard. But the system worked against them.

Table 2.1: Anatomy of a Missed Launch

Symptom	What It Looks Like	Root Systemic Cause
Slow Uptake	Market penetration lags forecasts despite solid clinical value	Static targeting; fragmented brand and field coordination
High Patient Abandonment	Significant drop-off before or shortly after therapy initiation	Reactive support timing; poor payer visibility; onboarding delays
Inconsistent Field Performance	Variable rep productivity across geographies or segments	Outdated segmentation; no integration with real-time signals
Underperforming Digital Channels	Low engagement rates, declining content consumption, lack of channel synergy	One-size-fits-all messaging; poor sequencing; channel silos
Escalating Spend, Weak ROI	Increased budget allocation but flat or negative ROI trendlines	Redundant efforts; lack of insight attribution across channels

In this model, even exceptional teams fail—because the structure they operate within is no longer fit for the challenge.

When the Numbers Tell the Story

We no longer need anecdotes. The data speaks clearly:

- **50%** of new product launches fail to meet first-year targets.

- Patients experience **3–6 weeks** of delay between prescription and therapy initiation.

- Only **20–30%** of HCP-targeted content drives meaningful engagement.

- Access friction is rising **faster** than field adaptation.

- **80%** of digital campaigns still rely on vanity metrics instead of outcomes.

This isn't a resource problem. It's a **relevance** problem.

This isn't a tech deficit. It's a **systems** issue.

Great products are being stalled—not by science but by fragmented, sluggish commercial execution.

The New Complexity

Commercialization is no longer a linear, rep-led process. It's a distributed, dynamic system—intersecting stakeholders, evolving access conditions, disparate channels, real-time signals, and regulatory pressures.

In the 1990s, success meant aligning a dozen reps with a message and a sample. Today, it means orchestrating activity across payer zones, IDNs, channel partners, and field, digital, and patient-facing platforms. The complexity curve isn't slowing. It's accelerating.

And yet, many commercial teams still operate as if it's 2005—relying on quarterly planning cycles, field-first sequencing, and top-down messaging that doesn't adapt once it leaves the MLR room.

The Field Has Changed—But the Support Hasn't

For years, the field force was the beating heart of pharma sales. But now, even the best reps are flying blind.

- Access to HCPs is declining—especially in key urban and institutional settings.

- Call plans are built quarterly—based on historical deciles, not real-time signals.

- Digital activity is disconnected—HCPs receive disjointed experiences.

- Reps lack insight into access updates, patient barriers, and behavior shifts.

- Managers are stuck in reporting loops instead of real-time coaching.

Table 2.2: How Commercial Stakeholders Have Evolved

Stakeholder	Then: 2005 Model	Now: 2025 Reality	New Implication
HCPs	Broad segments, frequent rep access	Precision segments, variable access, digital-first behaviors	Require dynamic targeting and hybrid engagement
Payers	Few national players, slow policy shifts	Dozens of regional formularies, real-time access changes	Need predictive access modeling and localized strategies
Field Force	Central to execution, analog call plans	Hybrid role with digital augmentation, limited face time	Field orchestration must be context-aware and signal-driven
Patients	Passive participants	Digitally savvy, financially burdened, information-seeking	Onboarding and support must be personalized and anticipatory
Provider Systems	Independent offices, little data integration	Consolidated IDNs, data-rich but access-controlled	Engagement must align to system priorities and data standards
Support Vendors	Fragmented handoffs	Integrated hubs with escalating service expectations	Coordination is key; orchestration

Today's reps don't need more direction. They need **better orchestration**.

Because success in the field isn't about effort alone, it's about **context**. And most field teams don't have it.

When Execution Outpaces Insight

This is another fault line—one of the most dangerous. Campaigns go live before they're validated. Messaging is optimized quarterly, not continuously. Field feedback comes anecdotally, filtered, and too late. Attribution often relies on correlation, not causation.

What's working? What's not? Why did performance dip? Was it access friction? Messaging fatigue? Market noise?

Most teams can't answer those questions with confidence. This means strategy starts to feel like guesswork—and guesswork doesn't scale, especially in environments where every lost week costs real patients, real opportunities, and real revenue.

The Real Cost of Waiting

It's tempting to delay transformation. It feels safer to tweak than to rebuild. To wait for more data. To defer until "after the next quarter."

But every day stuck in the old model carries a cost:

- Launch momentum erodes.
- HCP confidence stalls.
- Access barriers go unchallenged.
- Payers outmaneuver slow responses.
- Patients lose time—and sometimes lose trust.

And the longer we wait, the more we fall behind.

Not just behind competitors.

Behind the **science,** we're trying to commercialize. Because even the best therapy can fail to deliver impact—if the system bringing it to market wasn't designed for the complexity of today.

What Comes Next

The next part of this chapter will map the transition—what the new commercial system must be, why AI plays a central role, and how intelligent orchestration changes not just speed but precision, accountability, and outcomes.

Because this isn't about improving the old playbook; it's about building a new one—designed to learn, adapt, and deliver in real-time.

A system where commercial execution finally keeps pace with innovation. And where patients feel the difference. Because the solution isn't more content, it's not faster emails or another CRM add-on.

It's a new operating system—one that's responsive, predictive, orchestrated, accountable, and explainable by design. And in this system, intelligence isn't bolted on. It's **baked in**.

Rethinking What "Commercial Ready" Means

In the past, commercial readiness was a checklist:

- Brand plan?
- Messaging matrix?
- Field force trained?
- Digital assets approved?
- Launch campaign live?

But in today's market, those boxes don't guarantee traction.

Now, "ready" means something very different:

- Have we modeled real-world access barriers and payer shifts?

- Are HCPs being engaged based on real-time behavior, not historical segments?

- Are field reps empowered with live context, not stale call plans?

- Are patient services initiated **before** friction emerges?

- Is the system learning—daily, not quarterly?

Commercial readiness today is less about documentation—and more about **adaptation**.

Why AI—And Why Now?

Artificial intelligence isn't new to pharma. Many companies have experimented with AI in segmentation, targeting, or sales forecasting.

But those efforts have often been point solutions. Isolated. Departmental. Disconnected.

What we need now is not more AI pilots.

What we need is an **AI-native commercial system**—where intelligence flows through every function, coordinates every action and closes the gap between insight and execution.

The question isn't: *Should we use AI?*

It's: *How do we design a commercial system that learns and adapts every day?*

Tools Aren't Systems

This is where many organizations get stuck. They invest in sophisticated tools—and then layer them onto legacy systems.

The result? Faster dashboards. More dashboards. Beautiful dashboards, but the same lag. The same misalignment. The same slow decisions.

Table 2.3: Tools vs. Systems

Tools Dimension	Tools	Systems
Purpose	Improve isolated tasks or workflows	Coordinate complex, multi-channel operations
Scope	Departmental—marketing, field, analytics	Enterprise-wide—spanning brand, access, field, support
Action Orientation	Provide dashboards, alerts, and insights	Drive decisions, trigger actions, and adapt automatically
Learning Capability	Static unless reconfigured manually	Continuously learning from signal and performance
Dependency	Require human interpretation and orchestration	Operate semi-autonomously within rules and compliance boundaries
Integration Depth	Often layered onto legacy processes	Re-architect processes with intelligence at the core
Impact Measurement	Outputs (clicks, opens, visits)	Outcomes (time-to-therapy, refill adherence, patient conversion)

This isn't a tech gap. It's an architecture gap.

From Campaigns to Coordination

One of the most profound shifts is a mindset shift—from campaign-centric marketing to **continuous orchestration**. Traditionally, pharma teams have operated in a campaign rhythm:

- Awareness campaign.

- Adherence campaign.

- Access campaign.

- Education campaign.

Each is built separately. Each was measured in isolation. Each was lagging the market it was meant to serve. But here's the reality:

Doctors don't live in campaigns. Patients don't experience journeys one initiative at a time. Market signals don't align with quarterly reviews.

Coordination means breaking through that campaign mindset—and designing systems that sense, decide, and act across channels in real-time.

Because timing is everything, and coordination is the only way to stay relevant in a market that doesn't pause.

Measuring What Actually Matters

Along with new systems come new success metrics. Traditional KPIs—like call volumes, email opens, or TRx counts—don't capture modern performance.

In the AI Commercial Era, the most important questions sound more like this:

- Are we reducing time-to-therapy across priority segments?

- Are we predicting access friction before it slows adoption?

- Are reps adjusting based on signal, not schedule?

- Are patients receiving the right support at the right moment?

- Are our messages being tuned dynamically, not quarterly?

In other words, are we **orchestrating outcomes**, not just **measuring outputs**?

That's the shift. From passive measurement to active system learning.

Why Launchcode Was Built

As detailed in Chapter 1, Launchcode is a new kind of commercial infrastructure—built not just to support brand plans but to **replace** them with living systems.

What makes Launchcode different isn't that it uses AI. It's that it's structured **as a system**.

- It doesn't rely on campaign calendars—it reacts to market reality.

- It doesn't optimize in silos—it coordinates across functions.

- It doesn't offer dashboards—it delivers decisions.

Where most AI efforts try to retrofit intelligence into outdated frameworks, Launchcode was designed from the ground up to think.

That's the critical difference.

What Launchcode Solves	Legacy Result	With LaunchCode
Payer friction discovered post-launch	Access delays and patient dropout	Predictive modeling, proactive strategy
Content overload with no signal	Fatigue, low engagement	Adaptive sequencing, relevance scoring
Field reps flying blind	Inconsistent impact	Signal-based orchestration
Siloed brand/access/support activity	Fragmented HCP/patient experience	Real-time cross-functional coordination
Measurement based on lagging KPIs	Delayed or misaligned decisions	Real-time attribution and optimization

Launchcode isn't a better campaign tool.

It's a new commercial nervous system.

The Risk of Doing Nothing

Transformation always brings risk. But in this case, the bigger risk is inertia.

- A launch that misses its moment rarely recovers.
- An HCP who disengages is hard to win back.
- A patient who drops off therapy may never restart.
- A payer who locks you out doesn't revisit access easily.

Waiting feels cautious. But in the era of accelerated science, **waiting is the most expensive choice you can make**.

What Leaders Must Do Now

Commercial transformation won't come from IT or analytics alone. It requires leadership—visionary, pragmatic, and committed. If you're leading a brand, a commercial org, or a cross-functional team, here's what needs to happen now:

1. Admit that the system—not the people—is the constraint.

Stop blaming field performance or brand engagement. It's the architecture.

2. Redefine success metrics.

Move beyond TRx and message delivery to speed, adaptability, and coordinated impact.

3. Design for orchestration.

Integrate digital, field, access, and support—not just in meetings but in execution.

4. Invest in intelligent infrastructure.

Tools are not enough. Systems that learn and act are the future.

5. Create room for experimentation.

Launchcode isn't about perfection on day one. It's about learning faster than the competition.

This isn't about layering on more tech.

It's about reengineering how pharma works.

Looking Forward

In the chapters ahead, we'll go deeper into Launchcode:

- How each agent works—and how they coordinate?

- How compliance is embedded—not bolted on?

- How content, targeting, and rep activity are orchestrated?

- How performance is attributed, not assumed?

- And how to govern, scale, and measure success at the system level?

But here's the simple truth:

The old model broke because it couldn't keep up. The new model wins because it **never stops learning**. Commercial excellence in this era won't belong to the loudest voice or the biggest budget. It will belong to the most intelligent system—and the leaders willing to build it.

Chapter 3: AI in Action – Architecting the Intelligent Commercial System

Beyond Automation, Toward Intelligence

By now, the need for a smarter commercial model is no longer a hypothesis—it's a mandate. Complexity has eclipsed control. Campaigns can't keep pace. Field execution is out of sync with digital behavior. And dashboards, despite their polish, leave teams reacting instead of responding.

But what replaces the old machine isn't just a better dashboard or a faster call plan. It's something more foundational.

What's emerging is a new commercial architecture—less like a command-and-control operating model and more like a **responsive commercial nervous system**. And at the heart of that system is a new class of actors: the **intelligent agent**.

These aren't glorified workflows or task bots. They are dynamic, autonomous entities—each designed to sense the environment, make decisions, take action, and learn. Continuously.

That's not a tech upgrade. That's a **paradigm shift**.

Not Just Smarter Tools—Smarter Systems

Most commercial teams have already adopted some form of automation. Emails are scheduled. Campaigns are tracked. Call notes are logged. But automation isn't intelligence. Automation gets things done. Intelligence decides **what** should be done, **when**, and **why**.

Table 3.1: Automation vs. Intelligent Agent – A Shift from Tasks to Intelligence

Capability	Automation Tools	Intelligent Agents
Primary Function	Execute predefined tasks efficiently	Pursue commercial outcomes through adaptive decision-making
Decision Logic	Hard-coded workflows	Dynamic models driven by real-time signals and rules
Responsiveness	Triggered by static events	Continuously interpret signals and optimize responses
Learning & Adaptation	None or limited	Ongoing learning from feedback, performance, and evolving conditions
Governance & Oversight	Requires constant human review	Operates within guardrails—logged, explainable, auditable
Typical Use Cases	Email blasts, CRM updates, task reminders	Real-time HCP targeting, content sequencing, access response coordination
Strategic Impact	Efficiency gains within workflows	System-wide orchestration, measurable business impact

Intelligent agents don't just execute tasks—they **pursue outcomes**. They're not faster doers. They're smarter actors, purpose-built for the pace and friction of modern pharma.

What Is an Intelligent Agent?

Let's ground the concept.

An **intelligent agent** is an autonomous system that operates within a defined commercial environment. It ingests signals, evaluates options, and acts in pursuit of a specific outcome—whether that's increasing HCP engagement, reducing patient abandonment, or accelerating time to therapy.

Core characteristics of an intelligent agent:

1. **Goal-Oriented** – Operates with a clearly defined objective.

2. **Signal-Responsive** – Ingests real-time and historical data.

3. **Decision-Making** – Selects optimal actions from permitted options.

4. **Executable** – Connects with systems to act without human handoff.

5. **Self-Optimizing** – Learns from impact and adjusts logic accordingly.

This isn't theoretical. It's **operational cognition**—a structure that thinks and adapts faster than any brand plan ever could.

From Static Workflows to Living Systems

Traditional workflows were built on repetition and scale. If something worked, you did more of it—across reps, across markets, across time, but today's environment punishes sameness. Success depends on adaptability. This is why intelligent agents are built as **modular systems** with four essential components:

1. A Defined Commercial Objective

Every agent begins with a goal: increase engagement in a priority segment, reduce access friction in a target region, improve onboarding adherence for a new product.

This is not just task management. It's purpose-driven architecture.

2. A Set of Data Signals

Agents ingest a blend of live and historical data—EMR prescribing behavior, formulary shifts, hub enrollment patterns, field call notes, and patient drop-off rates.

But they don't just collect data—they interpret it. The signal becomes a story.

3. A Decision-Making Engine

Using machine learning models, business rules, and contextual thresholds, the agent evaluates potential actions:

- Should we adjust the rep call plan?
- Should we trigger a new patient education module?
- Should we suppress a fatigued message variant?

It selects the optimal path based on what it sees **and what it's learned**.

4. An Execution Path

Then comes action. The agent connects to commercial systems—CRMs, campaign platforms, patient support hubs—and executes. No ticketing. No approvals. Just governed action.

And when done, it evaluates impact—and starts again.

How Agents Learn (and Why That Matters)

At the core of every agent is a feedback loop.

Every action has a measurable outcome:

- Did engagement improve?
- Did the HCP prescribe?

- Did patient abandonment drop?

- Did access barriers shift?

If the outcome is positive, the agent strengthens that pathway. If not, it adjusts—or flags for human review.

Over time, agents learn to:

- Identify high-leverage actions for specific segments.

- Recognize signal patterns that predict friction.

- Allocate resources more precisely across the system.

This is not optimization once a quarter.

It's **self-tuning**, grounded in **real-world performance**, running every hour of every day.

Governance Without Guesswork

Understandably, many commercial leaders ask: *If these agents are autonomous... who's steering the ship?*

The answer? **Guardrails**—not guesswork.

Every intelligent agent in Launchcode operates within a clearly defined compliance perimeter:

- **Content libraries** are modular, pre-approved, and tagged.

- **Targeting thresholds** are enforced by business rules.

- **Patient outreach** is governed by consent, clinical policy, and frequency limits.

- **Decision logs** are maintained for traceability and audit-readiness.

Every decision is:

Logged.
Explainable.
Auditable.
Bound by business and legal rules.

Autonomy doesn't mean anarchy. It means **efficiency with control**, **learning with compliance**, and **speed with transparency**.

A System That Thinks Together

While each agent delivers value on its own, the real power lies in **coordination**.

Imagine this:

- The **Targeting Agent** detects declining engagement in a key segment.

- The **Messaging Agent** identifies content fatigue.

- The **Access Agent** spots a new formulary restriction in that territory.

- The **Field Agent** recalibrates rep visits to emphasize access updates.

- The **Patient Agent** prepares support resources for newly impacted patients.

- The **Performance Agent** tracks the TRx lift in the following week.

No command center. No cross-functional scramble.

The system adapts—because the agents are **listening to each other**.

A Living Commercial Organism

If the old commercial model was a machine—fixed inputs, linear outputs—then the new model is more like a body:

- **Launchcode sets the intent**—like the brain issuing a command.

- **Agents sense conditions**—like nerves detecting pressure, heat, or movement.

- **Actions adjust**—like muscles calibrating based on weight or resistance.

- **Feedback loops inform the next move**—in real-time.

This isn't process automation. It's a **commercial adaptation**. Built for nuance. Built for scale. Built for speed.

Why This Architecture Changes Everything

This isn't hype.

Intelligent agents are already reshaping how commercial teams operate—right now.

They're reducing the time to therapy. They're improving message relevance. They're enabling reps to act on signals, not spreadsheets. They're helping brand leads stay ahead of payer shifts and patient dropouts.

And they're doing it **without hiring more people**, **building more slides**, or **sending more emails**. They're making the commercial system **smarter every day**.

When Commercial Execution Becomes Orchestration

You now understand how intelligent agents operate—how they ingest signals, pursue goals, take action, and learn. But

Launchcode isn't a single agent. It's a **network of agents**—each accountable for a core commercial function, working together in real-time.

These agents aren't features. They're not roles. They're modular, adaptive systems that form the spine of an intelligent commercial model.

In this chapter, we unpack each one: what it does, how it thinks, and what makes it fundamentally different from traditional functions.

Agent 1: The Targeting Agent

"Who should we prioritize—and why?"

Purpose

Continuously prioritize HCPs, systems, and accounts based on current opportunity, signal, and strategic goals.

Key Signals

- EMR prescribing trends.
- Referral behavior.
- Rep notes and visit outcomes.
- Digital engagement and responsiveness.
- Local access dynamics.

Primary Actions

- Dynamically updates HCP/account rankings.
- Flags rising influencers or prescribing shifts.
- Adjusts segmentation logic in-flight.

Business Impact

- Improves engagement precision.

- Reduces rep time spent on low-impact calls.

- Surfaces opportunities before competitors do.

What makes it different: It's not a static decile list. It's a constantly learning prioritization engine tuned to real-world signals.

Agent 2: The Messaging Agent

"What message should go to whom—and in what sequence?"

Purpose

Optimize message content, format, and delivery across channels for relevance, timing, and regulatory fit.

Key Signals

- Channel-level content engagement (open rates, video views, etc.).

- Objection types and rep-entered call feedback.

- Message variant performance by segment.

- Regulatory constraints and tagging.

Primary Actions

- Personalizes content sequencing per HCP segment.

- Suppresses or replaces low-performing assets.

- Aligns field and digital messaging to avoid channel clash.

Business Impact

- Drives message resonance.

- Reduces content fatigue.

- Increases engagement conversion.

What makes it different: The Messaging Agent doesn't just deliver—it adapts. It finds the message that works **now**, not last quarter.

Agent 3: The Access Agent

"What's changing in coverage—and how should we respond?"

Purpose

Continuously monitor payer behavior and preempt access friction across plans, geographies, and time.

Key Signals

- Formulary changes and PA edits.

- Claims rejections and hub enrollments.

- OOP cost changes.

- Regional policy shifts.

Primary Actions

- Predicts emerging access blocks.

- Triggers support resources preemptively.

- Notifies field and messaging agents of friction zones.

- Adjusts pull-through playbooks regionally.

Business Impact

- Reduces surprise friction at launch.

- Accelerates time-to-access for patients.

- Aligns access, brand, and field in real time.

What makes it different: Traditional access strategies react. The Access Agent predicts—and responds at system speed.

Agent 4: The Field Agent

"Where should reps go—and what should they say?"

Purpose

Coordinate field activity with live opportunity signals, access changes, and omnichannel sequences.

Key Signals

- Call notes and HCP responsiveness.

- HCP engagement in non-personal channels.

- Rep schedule constraints and compliance windows.

- Access and messaging agent inputs.

Primary Actions

- Optimizes call plans daily or weekly.

- Flags high-potential and under-engaged HCPs.

- Sequences rep visits to complement digital outreach.

- Alerts managers with coaching insights.

Business Impact

- Improves rep ROI and focus.

- Increases account coverage with fewer reps.

- Enhances omnichannel coordination.

What makes it different: This agent doesn't replace the manager—it augments their visibility, turning insight into impact.

Agent 5: The Patient Agent

"Where is the patient journey breaking—and how can we help?"

Purpose

Identify and resolve patient journey friction—from access to onboarding to refill adherence.

Key Signals

- Hub enrollment and abandonment rates.
- Education module engagement.
- Refill and persistence trends.
- Support team interaction timing.

Primary Actions

- Initiates onboarding workflows on Rx.
- Escalates drop-off risks early.
- Personalizes support channels and content.
- Connects patients to human teams when necessary.

Business Impact

- Improves adherence.
- Reduces early abandonment.
- Enhances patient satisfaction and therapy initiation rates.

What makes it different: Patient support becomes proactive—not reactive. Personalized. Timed. Relevant.

Agent 6: The Performance Agent

"What's working—and what should we do next?"

Purpose

Attribute commercial results to specific actions taken by agents—and optimize future logic.

Key Signals

- TRx/Nrx performance by segment.
- Message response curves.
- Field activity ROI.
- Access correlation with engagement shifts.
- Patient journey conversions.

Primary Actions

- Adjusts weights and priorities in other agents.
- Surfaces high-ROI sequences.
- Flags negative signals early.
- Powers scenario modeling for future planning.

Business Impact

- Improves system performance over time.
- Transforms insight into action.
- Enables intelligent experimentation.

What makes it different: It doesn't just measure. It tunes the machine while it's running.

Table 3.2: Agent Capabilities at a Glance

Agent	Primary Goal	Key Business Impact
Targeting	Prioritize HCPs and systems dynamically	Field efficiency, signal-driven segmentation
Messaging	Sequence and optimize message delivery	Relevance, content ROI, HCP engagement lift
Access	Anticipate and respond to payer shifts	Faster time-to-access, fewer surprises
Field	Align rep activity with live opportunity	Territory ROI, omnichannel consistency
Patient	Reduce friction in patient experience	Adherence, satisfaction, conversion retention
Performance	Attribute and optimize system logic	Continuous learning, strategic clarity

When the Agents Move as One

Each agent creates value on its own. But their coordination is where transformation truly happens.

Here's how it plays out:

1. **Access Agent** flags a formulary change in a major plan.

2. **Targeting Agent** adjusts HCP priorities in the affected geography.

3. **Messaging Agent** sequences access-specific content.

4. **Field Agent** reorders rep activity to prioritize education visits.

5. **Patient Agent** launches onboarding reinforcement for new patients.

6. **Performance Agent** tracks changes across prescribing, time-to-therapy, and refill rates.

No lag. No fire drills. No siloed teams. Just orchestrated an intelligent response.

What It Feels Like

For the **rep**, it feels like walking into the right room at the right time with the right message. For the **brand lead**, it feels like confidence—the system is adapting. For **compliance**, it feels like control—everything is traceable, governable, and explainable. For **leadership**, it feels like clarity—the right levers, visible and measurable.

Launchcode doesn't just make things faster. It makes the whole system **more aware**. And in a market that changes hourly, that awareness becomes your advantage.

What Comes Next

In the next set of chapters, we'll go deeper—agent by agent. You'll see how to design, deploy, and govern each one. You'll learn how to integrate them with existing systems and teams. And you'll understand how to scale orchestration while staying compliant, focused, and adaptive.

Chapter 4: The Targeting Agent

From Call Lists to Cognitive Prioritization

Before any message is sent, any rep deployed, or any campaign launched, one question underpins the entire commercial strategy:

Who should we engage—and when?

It sounds simple. But for decades, the answer has been based on habit, not intelligence.

Deciles. TRx tiers. Static personas. Gut feel. Quarterly updates. Outdated spreadsheets. Reps working call plans based on coverage, not context.

It worked well enough when the world moved slowly—when the top 20% of prescribers accounted for 80% of volume, and reps had time, access, and autonomy.

But that world is gone.

Today, therapies are more specialized, audiences are more elusive, payer policy and competitive activity shift weekly, rep access is fleeting, and every HCP has more digital touchpoints, more content, and less attention than ever before.

The old playbook assumes the market stands still. **But the market never stops moving.** That's why Launchcode starts with the **Targeting Agent**.

Why Targeting Must Change

Legacy targeting systems treat the past as a roadmap to the future. But prescribing volume is a **lagging indicator**—it tells you who did something, not who will.

What TRx lists don't reveal:

- Who's newly interested in your brand.
- Who's disengaging quietly.
- Who's facing payer friction.
- Who's on the cusp of prescribing.
- Who's shifting attention to a competitor.

Most importantly, they don't adapt when the story changes.

That's where the Targeting Agent comes in.

What the Targeting Agent Is—and What It's Not

The Targeting Agent isn't just a smarter decile engine.

It's a continuously learning, autonomous system designed to **sense opportunity in motion**, reprioritize outreach, and guide engagement based on **real-time signal**, not historical volume.

It doesn't build the perfect list once a quarter. It refines the right list **every day**. It doesn't guess. It detects. It doesn't manage quotas. It maximizes potential. It watches behavior. Interprets data. Scores intent. Suggests next moves. And evolves with every interaction.

Table 4.1: Static vs. Dynamic Targeting

Traditional Targeting

Attribute	Traditional Targeting	Targeting Agent (Launchcode)
Update Frequency	Quarterly or monthly	Daily, based on real-time signals
Data Source	Historical prescribing (TRx/NRx)	Behavioral, clinical, access, and digital signal
Segmentation Logic	Fixed tiers (e.g., deciles, ABC)	Fluid rankings, adaptive scoring
Feedback Mechanism	Manual or lagging	Continuous learning from performance and rep feedback
Execution Dependence	Requires rep interpretation and human adjustment	Autonomous prioritization within business-defined guardrails
Strategic Risk	High—may overlook rising or disengaging HCPs	Low—detects and responds to changes early

The Targeting Agent doesn't just help you reach the right people. It helps you reach them **before anyone else does.**

How the Targeting Agent Works

Like every intelligent agent in LaunchCode, the Targeting Agent operates in a **closed-loop system** that observes, acts, learns—and then acts better.

1. Signal Detection

What defines the Targeting Agent isn't just that it sees more—it sees **differently**. It captures subtle patterns across sources that typically live in silos:

- **EMR data**: new diagnostic codes, discontinued therapies, investigational trial participation.

- **Payer feeds**: abrupt uptick in prior auth denials, formulary changes, or policy reversals.

- **Digital breadcrumbs**: HCP downloads, e-Detail module completions, social signal around KOL presentations.

- **Field insights**: rep-submitted call notes, objections logged in CRM, rep-assessed interest scores.

- **Behavioral drift**: changes in response timing, content sequencing drop-offs, reduced open rates.

- **Network adjacency**: peer behavior patterns within provider networks, shared affiliations, regional symposia attendance.

Together, these signals form **early warning systems** for interest, fatigue, or friction—far earlier than TRx volume ever could.

2. Opportunity Modeling

It applies machine learning models and business rules to evaluate:

- Likelihood to prescribe.

- Relevance of messaging.

- Risk of disengagement.

- Competitive vulnerability.

- Influence over other prescribers.

3. Prioritization and Action

It recalibrates the target list in real-time—triggering:

- Call plan adjustments.

- Digital sequences.
- Rep alerts.
- Content personalization.
- Cross-agent orchestration when appropriate.

4. Feedback and Learning

It tracks what happens next:

- Did the rep connect?
- Did the HCP engage?
- Did behavior change?

This data is looped back into the model, refining logic, weights, and thresholds.

It gets smarter. Daily.

Real-World Example: Oncology, Accelerated

Imagine an oncology launch.

Traditionally:

- The targeting list is fixed pre-launch.
- Reps pursue the top 100 TRx writers.
- The list refreshes quarterly—if at all.

With the Targeting Agent:

- A rising oncologist is detected ordering a biomarker panel linked to your therapy.
- She downloads your trial design overview from a conference site.

- She's flagged by the agent for high-opportunity engagement.
- The Messaging Agent sequences efficacy content tied to her specialty.
- The Field Agent prioritizes her for an early visit with focused talking points.

Engagement happens fast.
Relevance is high.
No noise. No lag. No guesswork.

Rare Disease, Rare Signal

In rare diseases, where patient volumes are small and prescribing patterns are nonlinear, the Targeting Agent becomes indispensable.

What a human team might miss:

- Patterns of lab test ordering.
- Clusters of symptom codes.
- Cross-referral behavior to specialized centers.
- Changes in payer approvals for diagnostics.

The agent isn't just looking for activity. It's detecting intent.

In rare diseases, that difference can define the trajectory of a launch.

This is the shift—from **broad effort** to **signal-driven precision**.

What It Feels Like to the Field

For most reps, targeting has long felt like a quota system—not a precision strategy.

They're handed a call list, given a decile threshold, and expected to "hit coverage." They know that not all targets have high potential, but they lack the data—or authority—to push back.

What the Targeting Agent offers is **focus with confidence**.

Now, instead of spending two days chasing disengaged accounts, a rep sees:

- "Dr. Simmons just completed an online module on MOA mechanisms—schedule her soon."

- "Dr. Patel's practice dropped in formulary coverage this week—hold digital messaging until resolved."

- "Dr. Chou is newly seeing patients flagged with your target biomarkers—prioritize with field visit + access support."

This level of insight empowers reps to act smarter—not just harder. And for managers, it opens up a new mode of coaching:

- Which rep is acting on signal fastest?

- Where are reps overriding suggestions—and what can be learned?

- How is targeting precision correlating with TRx lift or pull-through acceleration?

In short, the field moves from **execution to orchestration**.

Rethinking Segmentation Itself

Most commercial teams segment HCPs by a persona:

- Specialty.

- Volume.

- Channel preference.

- Objection type.

But segmentation is inherently **static**.

The Targeting Agent adds what segmentation lacks: **temporal awareness**.

Table 4.2: Segmentation vs. Targeting Agent Prioritization Segmentation

Dimension	Segmentation (Traditional)	Targeting Agent (Launchcode)
Core Focus	Define audience personas	Prioritize specific HCPs/accounts for timely action
Time Sensitivity	Low—updated annually or semi-annually	High—updated daily or weekly based on evolving opportunity
Basis for Decision	Static attributes (specialty, TRx, preference)	Live behavior and environmental signals (access, digital, EMR)
Output	Channel or content alignment	Real-time engagement recommendation
Flexibility	Rigid categories	Adaptive, continuously re-ranked
Strategic Role	Determines "what to say"	Determines "who to engage now—and when"

Together, segmentation and dynamic targeting become a strategic pair: Segmentation tells you **what** to say.

- Targeting tells you **who to engage next—and when**.

When Targeting Goes Wrong

Targeting is often treated as an operational issue.

But when it's mismanaged, the consequences are strategic:

- **Wasted rep time** – Every low-opportunity call is a missed chance to engage someone else.

- **Lost HCP trust** – Reps delivering irrelevant messages are seen as noise, not value.

- **Delayed access** – Missing early signals from newly active HCPs means slower patient starts.

- **Budget inefficiency** – Campaigns misaligned with real opportunity drive up spending with no return.

- **Field frustration** – Reps working lists that don't align with on-the-ground reality become disengaged.

In highly competitive categories, **these misfires compound**. One missed HCP can shift prescribing patterns for a region. One mistimed message can delay therapy adoption by weeks. One underperforming segment can drag down an entire launch curve.

This is why targeting can no longer be static, broad, or assumption-based. It must be intelligent. Adaptive. And constantly evolving.

When Targeting Becomes the Catalyst

The real power of the Targeting Agent isn't just in smarter prioritization. It's in how that prioritization becomes a signal **for the rest of the system**. Because targeting is not a standalone function, it's a trigger.

It tells the Messaging Agent what to say.

It tells the Field Agent where to go.

It tells the Access Agent where friction might surface.

It alerts the Patient Agent to prepare support.

And it gives the Performance Agent a baseline to measure success.

In the world of Launchcode, targeting doesn't just identify "who." It sets the **orchestration in motion.**

Targeting as an Orchestration Trigger

Let's make this concrete.

Integrated Example: A Neurology Brand in Early Launch

A brand is launching a new therapy for treatment-resistant epilepsy. Here's how the Targeting Agent drives orchestration within the first 60 days:

- **Targeting Agent** identifies neurologists who:
- Show diagnostic activity related to the condition.
- Attended a recent MOA-focused congress session.
- Downloaded a clinical summary from the brand's microsite.
- These HCPs are re-prioritized based on engagement signal and projected coverage readiness.

Then, the system responds:

No one called a meeting. No one sent an email. The system aligned—because **targeting acted as a signal**, not just a spreadsheet.

Targeting Across the Product Lifecycle

One of the most overlooked advantages of the Targeting Agent is its ability to **evolve with the brand**. Different phases require different targeting logic. The agent adapts.

Table 4.3: Targeting Focus by Lifecycle Stage

Agent	Action Taken
Messaging Agent	Launches a tailored content sequence tied to the congress theme and MOA insights
Field Agent	Schedules rep visits where digital engagement is high but face-to-face is needed.
Access Agent	Models payer timelines to pace education around prior auth hurdles.
Patient Agent	Prepares onboarding materials for regions with fast initiation potential
Performance Agent	Monitors lift in TRx and time-to-engagement to validate and improve future cycles.

The agent isn't rebuilt each year.

It **grows with your product.**

Equity by Design

Traditionally, commercial targeting has unintentionally reinforced health disparities.

Volume-based targeting favors high-prescribing HCPs, who are often clustered in well-resourced geographies.

Underserved communities, community health centers, and rural prescribers often fall below the decile line—and are excluded entirely. The Targeting Agent creates an opportunity to change that.

Because it doesn't just score on TRx. It scores on the **signal**:

- Emerging activity in underserved regions.
- Digital engagement from community-based providers.
- Patients need patterns, not just prescribing history.
- Signs of delayed access or systemic friction.

By designing equity into the scoring logic—intentionally—the agent can:

- Surface HCPs who are disproportionately important to underserved patients.
- Flag geographic blind spots before they become health outcome gaps.
- Expand access with precision, not just scale.

Health equity isn't a compliance issue.

It's a design choice. And intelligent systems make that choice possible.

Measuring What Matters

Targeting isn't just a strategy—it's a performance lever. And it has to be **measured** as such.

All of these metrics flow into the Performance Agent, which doesn't just report—they **course correct**.

Trust, Transparency, and Adoption

Like any AI system, the Targeting Agent is only valuable if people **trust it**. Trust is built on visibility.

Launchcode makes every targeting decision:

- **Explainable** – each HCP score can be unpacked into contributing factors.

- **Auditable** – all recommendations and actions are logged.

- **Governed** – with frequency limits, exclusion logic, and override capabilities.

- **Interactive** – reps and managers can provide feedback that improves the system.

When field teams **see the "why"** behind each target—and that their input matters—they don't just adopt the agent.

They advocate for it.

From Strategy to System

In traditional commercialization, targeting was a planning function. In the AI Commercial Era, targeting is a **living system**—constantly sensing, interpreting, and influencing the entire commercial engine.

It becomes:

- A **strategic control panel** for the launch.

- A **focus amplifier** for the field.

- A **signal trigger** for messaging.

- An **early alert** for access and patient teams.

- A **feedback loop** for continuous system learning.

And over time, it doesn't just improve execution.

It shapes how brands respond to the market—**in real-time, at scale.**

Final Thought

Most teams treat targeting as the first step in execution. But in Launchcode, it's the first step in **orchestration**. It doesn't just tell you where to go.

It gets you there faster. With more relevance. Less friction. And measurable impact.

Because in today's environment, the companies that win aren't the ones with the best call list. They're the ones with the best system—for knowing who matters most **right now.**

Chapter 5: The Messaging Agent

From Push to Precision

Why Messaging Matters More Than Ever

For decades, pharma believed the path to influence was paved with consistency and frequency. Teams built exhaustive message matrices, trained reps to deliver the same core claims, and flooded HCPs with omnichannel campaigns calibrated for share of voice. But that formula no longer holds.

Today, HCP inboxes are flooded. Their attention is fragmented. And their tolerance for irrelevant, duplicative, or poorly timed content is at an all-time low.

It's no longer about what you say. It's about **when, how,** and **in what order** you say it. And most importantly—**to whom.**

In a world where every click, view, or referral sends a signal, pharma messaging must shift from static delivery to dynamic orchestration.

That's the role of the **Messaging Agent.**

Why the System Is Broken

At many pharma companies, messaging still lives in disconnected silos:

- Brand teams define core messages months in advance.

- Digital teams launch campaigns on fixed calendars.

- Field teams are briefed on "key points" but left to adapt on the fly.

- Compliance teams enforce uniformity by limiting experimentation.

The result?

A flood of content that may be accurate—but is rarely aligned, timely, or calibrated for individual needs.

Many brand teams assume that if an HCP receives five exposures to a message, they must be getting the point.

But here's what that looks like from the HCP side:

- An email about efficacy.

- A rep visited about safety.

- A portal banner about access.

- A webinar that repeats the efficacy.

- A follow-up email that leads with the cost.

Each message might be useful—but the **narrative arc is broken**. And in a market flooded with options, a broken narrative is a lost opportunity.

The Collapse of Traditional Messaging

Legacy systems were built for delivery, not adaptation. They treated messaging as a checklist: approve the core claims, adapt for the channel, and deploy on schedule.

But in practice, this approach creates friction for HCPs and waste for brands.

Common breakdowns include:

- **Static message grids**: Built months in advance, unresponsive to evolving signal.

- **Channel fragmentation**: Digital and field messages operate in silos, often duplicating or contradicting each other.

- **Lack of sequencing**: Messages arrive out of order, confusing rather than persuading.

- **No real testing**: Most brands don't know which message works best for which HCP type.

- **Slow optimization**: Content refreshes happen quarterly, driven by opinion, not performance.

The shift isn't digital. It's directional—from broadcasting messages to orchestrating moments of influence.

Table 5.1: Traditional Messaging vs. Launchcode Messaging Agent

Capability	Traditional Messaging	Messaging Agent (Launchcode)
Message Selection	Based on static playbooks and TRx segmentation	Driven by real-time behavior, signal, and engagement context
Content Deployment	Uniforms across audience segments	Personalized by clinical profile, digital behavior, and channel preference
Testing & Optimization	Ad hoc, limited to major campaigns	Continuous A/B and multivariate testing at the message and sequence level
Sequencing Strategy	Rarely implemented or enforced.	Dynamically modeled to reflect timing, behavior phase, and cognitive patterns.
Field Integration	Informational: The rep chooses from general themes	Coordinated with Field Agent and tailored to rep-HCP interaction history
Refresh Cycle	Quarterly or brand milestone-driven	Daily to weekly adjustments based on real-time feedback

What Is the Messaging Agent?

The Messaging Agent is an autonomous learning system designed to determine **what message to deliver**, **to whom**, **through which channel**, **in what order**, and **at what moment**.

Its Mission:

1. **Maximize message relevance** – Match content to behavior, specialty, and engagement signal.

2. **Optimize sequencing** – Ensure each message builds on the last, not competes with it.

3. **Personalize delivery** – Adapt format, cadence, and timing based on individual HCP needs.

4. **Learn what works** – Continuously test, evaluate, and refine content effectiveness.

5. **Coordinate channels** – Sync field, digital, and peer-delivered messaging into a unified arc.

This is not just content distribution. It's **commercial cognition** at the messaging level.

The Engine Behind the Agent

The Messaging Agent operates through a five-step loop:

1. Ingest Modular Content

Pre-approved, modular messages are tagged by:

- Audience segment.

- Indication/disease stage.

- Access scenario.

- Format (email, banner, video, rep detail).

- Behavior trigger.

- Risk/compliance status.

2. Analyze Signal

For each HCP or segment, the agent scans:

- Digital engagement behavior (opens, clicks, page depth).

- Rep interaction history and objections.

- Access environment (payer approvals, hub data).

- Clinical behavior (TRx trends, diagnosis codes).

- Channel preference and frequency tolerance.

3. Select and Sequence

The system selects:

- The most relevant message for the moment.

- The appropriate format (visual, text, rep-detail).

- A supporting message sequence for continuity.

- Suppression or escalation based on recent exposure.

4. Deploy Across Channels

Content is activated via:

- CRM and field tools.

- Email platforms.

- Portals and banners.

- Microsites and educational webinars.

5. Evaluate and Adjust

The agent evaluates:

- Clicks, views, and dwell time.

- Behavioral response (prescription, referrals, follow-up actions).

- Drop-off thresholds and saturation risk.

- Variant lift by HCP type or region.

The result: a system that **thinks before it speaks**—and learns every time it does.

The Power of Sequence

Messaging isn't just about **content**—it's about **context over time**.

A great message, poorly timed, loses its power. A correct claim, repeated too often, becomes background noise. But sequenced well, messages tell a story—one that builds understanding, trust, and action.

Consider this example:

- **Incorrect sequence**: Access message → efficacy → patient impact.

- **Optimized sequence**: Efficacy → safety → access → patient impact.

In the optimized flow, the HCP sees evidence, reassurance, logistics, and outcomes—in a psychologically aligned path.

This isn't random—it's behavioral science:

- **Primacy and recency**: The first and last messages carry more weight.

- **Cognitive load**: Too many messages too fast reduces retention.

- **Emotional resonance**: Sequencing can increase confidence or urgency based on message order.

The Messaging Agent models sequence lift and adjust paths by:

- Engagement phase.

- Specialty.

- Access scenario.

- Regional saturation.

- Peer-to-peer exposure.

Message order matters as much as message content.

Use Case: Immunology in Action

A new biologic enters a crowded autoimmune category. Brand teams expect slow uptake due to entrenched competition.

The Messaging Agent:

- Detects high interest in efficacy visuals but fatigue on access content.

- Adjusts sequences to prioritize peer-led safety messaging.

- Identifies that engagement rises when rep visits follow digital education within 3 days.

- Retires low-performing message variants.

- Coordinates with the Field Agent for in-person follow-up using aligned themes.

Result:

- Engagement rates increase by **18%**

- Pre-call objections drop by **20%**

- Net prescribing lifts **15% in 8 weeks**—without additional field force or spend

The insight? Great content helps. Sequenced, coordinated, data-informed messaging performs.

Personalization Without Chaos

The phrase "personalized messaging" often triggers concern in compliance meetings.

How do you personalize content **without creating a regulatory nightmare**?

The Messaging Agent solves this through **governed modularity**:

- All content variants are pre-reviewed.

- Tags and logic—not rewrites—drive personalization.

- Every delivered message is logged and versioned.

- Escalation rules are hard-coded (e.g., frequency limits, safety flag triggers).

- Reps are only shown approved permutations aligned to their call plans.

Example in Practice:

- Dr. Lin is a GI specialist with prior exposure to a core safety message.

- The agent detects that she clicked on a peer case study last week.

- A new message sequence is deployed: peer experience → local access alert → patient onboarding tip.

- Each module is drawn from pre-approved content blocks.

- The sequence is reviewed by compliance quarterly—but optimized weekly based on the signal.

The result is not chaos. It's controlled variation—traceable, explainable, and safe.

Because in this era, messaging is no longer a marketing function.

It's a **system-level lever**.

Precision Content in a Dynamic System

Messaging Is Not a Solo Act

No matter how precise the message, timing and context determine whether it lands—or falls flat.

That's why the Messaging Agent doesn't operate in isolation. It functions as part of the broader **Launchcode orchestration network**—learning, signaling, and adjusting in coordination with the other five intelligent agents. It doesn't just ask, "What should we say?"

It asks:

"What should we say, to whom, through which channel, at what moment—based on everything else the system knows?"

And once the message is delivered, it learns from the response, adjusts the plan, and updates the system.

The Agent Ecosystem in Action

Let's revisit a real-world scenario: an endocrinology brand managing a complex launch for a GLP-1 therapy.

Here's how the Messaging Agent works within the network:

- **Targeting Agent** flags a set of HCPs engaging heavily with disease education content but showing no prescribing activity.

- **Messaging Agent** selects a tailored sequence focused on safety, peer case studies, and emerging real-world evidence.

- **Field Agent** aligns rep visits three days post-content exposure, ensuring timing enhances—not interrupts—engagement.

- **Access Agent** detects payer restrictions in the region and triggers supplemental messaging that clarifies coverage and prior auth pathways.

- **The Patient Agent** prepares onboarding materials and schedules support for once prescribing begins.

- **Performance Agent** evaluates lift from the entire coordinated effort, feeding signal back into the messaging logic.

This isn't multichannel execution. It's **intelligent orchestration**.

When the Message Misses the Mark

Even good content can fail. Sometimes the message is right, but:

- It arrives **too early** in the HCP's decision cycle.

- It's **redundant** with what the HCP just heard from a rep.

- It's **technically accurate** but lacks **emotional resonance.**

- It **assumes access is resolved** when it's not.

- It hits the **right point** but in the **wrong format.**

In traditional systems, these nuances go undetected.

In Launchcode, the Messaging Agent flags underperformance, tests alternatives, suppresses fatigue-inducing content, and rewires sequences—not just swap assets.

Table 5.2: Common Messaging Failure Modes—And How the Agent Responds

Failure Mode	Agent Response
Content fatigue	Rotates format suppresses overused messages or shifts to alternate themes
Misaligned sequence	Reorders content based on HCP behavior stage or prior message exposure
Off-topic objections	Adjusts next message based on rep feedback and digital objection tagging
Engagement drop-off	Modifies cadence, reduces message frequency, or switches to less intrusive formats
Channel mismatch	Redirects content to preferred format (e.g., email → rep detail or webinar invite)

The Messaging Agent doesn't just detect breakdowns—it self-corrects in real-time.

What It Feels Like to the Field

In most organizations, reps feel like messaging happens *to them*, not *with them*.

They're handed detail aids. Told to "emphasize this claim." Asked to follow up on campaigns they didn't know were running.

With the Messaging Agent, that disconnect disappears. Reps experience messaging as a **co-pilot**, not a command center:

- Their daily schedule reflects what content the HCP has already seen.

- Prep materials suggest **which messages to lead with**, based on signal.

- Objection management is dynamic—drawing from a growing set of pre-approved responses tailored to the HCP's behavior.

- They can flag what *didn't work* in a call—and know that the system will listen, adjust, and learn.

For the rep, LaunchCode messaging feels like:

- "You've got my back."

- "You know what my customer just saw."

- "I don't have to repeat. I can deepen."

- "I'm not guessing. I'm sequencing."

From Creative Factory to Strategic Asset

Creative teams often feel like they're drowning in versioning, formatting, and cross-functional firefighting. But the Messaging Agent redefines their value—not as content producers, but as **experience designers**.

The shift looks like this:

1. Modularization

Messages are developed as interoperable blocks—headlines, visuals, pull-throughs—that can be reused and recombined.

2. Metadata Tagging

Every content module is enriched with tags: topic, tone, audience, sequence fit, access context, risk category.

3. Structured Experimentati

Instead of one approved message, multiple variants are tagged and tested by the system—with performance feedback scaling the winners.

Creative teams move from reactive production to proactive system architecture.

Use Case: Rare Disease Storytelling

Rare disease launches face three critical constraints:

1. Limited prescriber base.

2. High information complexity.

3. Urgent need for trust.

In a recent neuromuscular launch, the Messaging Agent operated like a narrative guide:

- **Week 1**: Introduced clinical signs and diagnostic cues through visual cases.

- **Week 2**: Followed up with MOA + safety profile once the HCP engaged twice.

- **Week 3**: Delivered peer KOL stories segmented by setting. (academic vs. community)

- **Week 4**: Timed localized access messaging to coincide with payer policy updates.

- **Week 5**: Triggered rep visits to reinforce messages and close decision gaps.

The Messaging Agent didn't push content. It **paced a conversation**.

Beyond Clicks: Measuring What Matters

Traditional measurement relies on the following:

- Open rates.

- Clicks.

- Page views.

- Script lift. (if lucky)

But these don't capture narrative influence or sequence intelligence.

Table 5.3: Next-Gen Messaging Metrics

Metric	What It Reveals
Sequence lift	How message order influences engagement, action, or TRx
Variant performance	Which message versions perform best by segment, region, or specialty
Attention decay curve	How long HCPs stay engaged before drop-off—by sequence and channel
Channel-content fit	Which content types are best suited for each delivery format
Rep-digital alignment score	How well field and digital engagements reinforce one another

These metrics feed into the **Performance Agent**, enabling system-wide content optimization.

Governance at Speed

Dynamic messaging doesn't mean wild messaging.

The Messaging Agent operates within a **rules-based, auditable framework**:

- All content is versioned, tagged, and pre-reviewed.

- Sequencing rules are embedded in system logic.

- Frequency caps and suppression thresholds are hard-coded.

- Escalation triggers prompt real-time compliance involvement.

Compliance isn't a gatekeeper. It's a **design partner**.

Messaging Beyond HCPs

Though this chapter focuses on prescribers, the Messaging Agent also supports **patient communication** via the Patient Agent.

Function	Strategic Impact
Message selection	Improves personalization, HCP relevance, and early-stage resonance
Sequencing	Enhances clarity, retention, and behavioral lift
Multichannel alignment	Ensures consistency across digital, field, peer, and support channels
Performance feedback	Enables adaptive learning and system-wide message improvement
Creative transformation	Reduces content waste and improves ROI on modular content investments
Compliance governance	Maintains auditability, frequency control, and risk management at scale

It ensures:

- Patient messages align with what HCPs have seen.

- Educational materials are timed with prescription and onboarding moments.

- Format and tone adjust to literacy, digital comfort, and emotional context.

It doesn't just communicate. It **guides experience.**

Table 5.4: Messaging Agent Strategic Value

Final Thought

In the old model, messaging was a campaign: scheduled, siloed, and static. In the new model, **messaging is a system—**

alive, adaptive, and accountable. The Messaging Agent doesn't just help you deliver the right message. It helps you deliver it to the right person through the right channel at the right moment—**And learn from the outcome every single time.**

This is not automation for the sake of efficiency. It's orchestration in service of impact. Because in the AI Commercial Era, it's not enough to be heard.

You need to be relevant—**again and again.**

Chapter 6: The Access Agent

Navigating the New Terrain of Market Access

Why Access Is Everyone's Problem Now

It wasn't long ago that market access was viewed as a specialized function—a department downstream from launch planning, mostly focused on formulary negotiations and supporting pull-through. Once the coverage battle was won, access became background noise. Commercial energy shifted to sales force execution, brand messaging, and HCP engagement.

But today, access is no longer an edge case. It's the main event. Every commercial function now feels the pressure of access friction:

- **Targeting suffers** when high-potential HCPs are blocked by payer restrictions.

- **Messaging misfires** when content doesn't reflect the reality of coverage.

- **Field teams disengage** when objections are driven by benefit design, not clinical doubt.

- **Patient journeys stall** due to co-pay spikes, specialty pharmacy confusion, or delays in prior auth.

Payers no longer simply approve or deny. They shape adoption curves.

They dictate patient timelines. And increasingly, they define commercial outcomes.

Access has become everyone's business.

And as payers grow more aggressive in implementing utilization management strategies, brands are feeling the squeeze—not just at launch but across the lifecycle. Even established therapies now face new restrictions mid-year, driven by rebating wars or shifting formulary priorities. That means no brand is immune—and no team can afford to ignore what's happening at the access layer.

The New Rules of Friction

Access today is a mosaic of inconsistency:

- In one region, therapy may be Tier 2 with no prior authorization.

- One county over, it requires multiple-step edits, manual PA forms, and specialty distribution.

- Some payers accept digital submissions. Others reject anything that's not on their portal.

- Patients with the same insurance plan may face radically different out-of-pocket costs based on provider network, geography, or fulfillment channel.

And these variables shift constantly:

- Coverage rules change mid-year.

- Benefit verification cycles lag.

- Formularies get reshuffled with little notice.

What that creates isn't just **complexity**. It's **uncertainty**.

Uncertainty erodes:

- **Prescriber confidence.** ("Will my patient be covered?")

- **Patient trust.** ("Why is this so hard to get?")

- **Field efficiency.** ("What should I even say right now?")

The downstream effects are easy to miss unless you're watching closely. For example:

- Reps may deprioritize high-value prescribers because of assumed access challenges.

- Digital open rates may drop due to perceived coverage fatigue.

- High-need patients may abandon therapy altogether after one failed pickup.

That's why today's commercialization leaders can't afford to treat access as a checkbox. It's not just about getting on the formulary. It's about making sure every stakeholder—from rep to patient—can confidently navigate the journey.

The Lag Time Problem

In most pharma organizations, the playbook for addressing access barriers looks like this:

1. Field reports a problem.

2. Market access investigates.

3. Hub data is reviewed.

4. A payer team is looped in.

5. Messaging is crafted.

6. MLR approves content.

7. A resource is published.

8. Field teams are notified.

Time elapsed: 4–6 weeks.

Meanwhile:

- Prescriptions are lost.

- HCPs switch therapies.

- Patients fall out of the funnel.

The consequence isn't just a delay. It's a breakdown in momentum—often unrecoverable.

Table 6.1: Traditional Access Strategy vs. Access Agent Response

Aspect	Traditional Approach	Access Agent Approach
Response Time	Weeks post-signal	Real-time alert and system response
Signal Detection	Field anecdote or manual hub analysis	Predictive, geography-level, and payer-specific signal
Action Initiation	Manual, via payer/brand escalation	Autonomous triggering across field, content, and patient support
System Integration	Fragmented or disconnected	Embedded in CRM, hub, targeting, and messaging agents
Adaptability	Static playbooks	Dynamic adjustment to changing access conditions

Access isn't a workflow to manage. It's a signal to orchestrate around.

Meet the Access Agent

The Access Agent is Launchcode's intelligent response to payer complexity. It's not just a data layer or dashboard. It's a signal engine—an always-on, always-adapting actor that:

1. Monitors access behavior across payers, geographies, and time.

2. Detects and simulates access friction before field teams report it.

3. Trigger mitigation actions: messaging updates, field alignment, and patient support.

4. Integrates payer signals back into targeting and onboarding workflows.

5. Coordinates with other agents to turn payer risk into system responsiveness.

It's not passive tracking. It's proactive orchestration.

The goal isn't simply faster insights. It's better timing, smarter targeting, and more confident execution. The Access Agent ensures that when friction emerges, the entire commercial system knows how to respond—and does so without waiting for a war room.

How It Works

The Access Agent ingests data across four core dimensions:

- **Structured Data**: PA rules, formulary status, plan tiers, hub activity logs.

- **Behavioral Data**: Script abandonment, call notes, digital friction.

- **Predictive Models**: Payer responsiveness by geography, product analogs, and specialty trends.

- **Compliance Logic**: Guardrails for content updates, support triggers, and rep notification thresholds.

Every access event is interpreted as a signal:

- What changed?

- Who is affected?

- Where is momentum at risk?

- What coordinated actions can reduce drop-off?

And then it acts.

By integrating these signals with the other Launchcode agents, the Access Agent ensures that the brand's access reality isn't something teams stumble into—it's something they prepare for, align around, and respond to with speed.

Scenario: MigraRelief Hits a Formulary Wall

A real-world illustration:

- MigraRelief, a new migraine therapy, loses Tier 2 status on a major Mid-Atlantic plan.

- The Access Agent detects increased rejections and longer hub processing times.

- It maps the change to ZIP codes and identifies affected HCPs.

- Field Agent updates rep schedules.

- Messaging Agent deploys region-specific access content.

- Patient Agent prepares cost and support messaging on branded portals.

All within 24 hours of the change.

What once took weeks of reactive coordination is now an orchestrated, system-wide response. And that response isn't just about mitigating damage—it's about preserving momentum. The field is prepared, the HCP is informed, and the patient is reassured. That's the power of orchestration in action.

Access as a Targeting Signal

Access signal isn't just for payer teams.

- HCPs experiencing friction often deprioritize prescribing.

- Reps may skip accounts without realizing the friction is resolvable.

- Digital engagement can decline due to access-based disillusionment.

That's why the Access Agent feeds into the Targeting Agent:

- **HCP prioritization** adapts to real-time access shifts.

- **Territory focus** realigns to zones of pull-through opportunity.

- **Rep routes** adjust to focus where effort can lead to action.

It also helps avoid misalignment. Instead of asking reps to push in territories where coverage has just tightened, it shifts effort toward segments and geographies where scripts are most likely to be filled.

Access isn't just a cost. It's a constraint that reshapes the commercial map.

From Detection to Prediction

What makes the Access Agent truly transformative is its ability to simulate friction before it hits.

- Predicts likely barriers for new launches using analog products.

- Models payer adoption curves by region.

- Identifies "access deserts" where pathways are complex and coverage is weak.

- Forecasts abandonment risk by co-pay level, specialty pharmacy delays, or prior auth burden.

This enables brands to prepare:

- Regional messaging strategies **in advance**.

- Rep training tailored to access objections.

- Onboarding workflows optimized for early friction points.

It turns market access into a **strategic asset**—a source of foresight, not fire drills.

No more reacting to the fire. You're preventing it before it starts. From Market Hurdle to Strategic Advantage

Enabling Equitable Access

Access isn't just a commercial challenge. It's a healthcare equity issue.

Too often, systemic barriers to access disproportionately affect underserved populations:

- Lower-income patients face higher co-pays and fewer financial support options.

- Rural geographies lack proximity to specialty pharmacies or care coordination hubs.

- Language and health literacy gaps impede the navigation of complex access processes.

- Smaller provider practices may not have staff to manage benefits or pursue appeals.

The Access Agent can't fix structural inequity alone, but it can:

- Detect where friction is concentrated.

- Identify populations most at risk of falling through the cracks.

- Trigger-tailored, language-appropriate education modules.

- Prompt escalation to human support teams for high-risk patients.

This functionality is especially critical in therapeutic areas like oncology, endocrinology, and rare disease—where the burden of navigating access can create unacceptable disparities in time-to-therapy. The Access Agent turns reactive efforts into proactive equity infrastructure.

Table 6.2: Access Agent Contributions to Health Equity

Barrier	Agent Response
High co-pay burden	Auto-enrolls patients in co-pay support triggers early communication.
Rural or underserved region	Alerts field/hub teams prioritizes simplified onboarding workflows.
Language or literacy gap	Surfaces translated content and reduces jargon in educational materials.
Practice-level limitations	Pushes guided PA support escalates non-digital submissions automatically.

Equity doesn't just require outreach. It requires friction reduction. And the Access Agent makes that measurable.

Field Coordination in Real Time

Traditionally, field teams operate from call plans shaped by decile data and historical prescribing behavior. But those models ignore real-time payer friction.

The Access Agent fixes that.

When coverage shifts, it:

- Identifies affected HCPs.

- Updates rep schedules.

- Provides talking points and access-approved messaging.

- Notifies managers for coaching alignment.

This coordination doesn't stop at the territory level. It informs weekly district planning, salesforce resource allocation, and even home office escalation procedures. Managers no longer rely solely on rep anecdotes or territory guesswork—they act on signal.

Table 6.3: Access Signal to Field Flow

Access Event	Rep Enablement
Formulary downgrade	Updates call plans and adds payer-specific messaging modules.
PA implemented mid-cycle	Sends real-time alerts, provides objection handling resources
High-rejection ZIP codes	Flags urgent visits, syncs field + digital pull-through content
Spike in cost-based dropout	Triggers messaging + hub escalation for cost education

The result? Reps walk in prepared, not blindsided. And brand momentum stays intact.

Patient Experience Reinvented

Access friction is the #1 reason patients abandon treatment. And it often happens silently:

- They hit a coverage delay and never called back.

- A surprise co-pay discourages fulfillment.

- They get no follow-up after denial.

The Access Agent works hand-in-hand with the Patient Agent to eliminate these dead ends:

- **Hub delays** trigger automated updates + education.

- **High co-pays** launch co-pay program workflows.

- **PA denials** push escalation logic to support teams.

- **Digital silence** prompts multi-channel reminders.

It also identifies moments where a single nudge can make all the difference:

- Sending a follow-up message when a benefit verification stalls.

- Offering a cost calculator after a rejected claim.

- Reassuring a patient about the next steps before treatment abandonment.

This is what it means to operationalize empathy.

And because every interaction is logged, the brand doesn't just fix problems—it learns where patient journeys are breaking and how to design better experiences next time.

Competitive Defense in Access Battles

The Access Agent isn't just reactive to your brand's friction. It watches the competitive environment, too.

Here's how:

- Monitors payer updates across therapeutic classes.

- Flags drop in approval rates that correlate to competitive wins.

- Surfaces HCPs in high-risk churn zones.

- Aligns counter-detailing content (differentiation, real-world evidence).

- Prepares reps with objection-handling scripts and hub support options.

The result is a defense strategy that's fast, precise, and coordinated across the system.

This also allows earlier detection of formulary displacement, rebating shifts, or tier migration that could compromise first-line prescribing status. Rather than discover competitive movement through TRx loss, brands can intervene before market share slips.

Launch Readiness with Access at the Center

Let's walk through a launch simulation:

A monoclonal antibody is preparing to enter a competitive immunology category. The Access Agent is deployed 60 days pre-launch to:

- Simulate likely payer adoption curves.

- Forecast formulary tiers and required documentation.

- Model time-to-therapy delays by geography and provider type.

- Identify ZIP codes likely to become coverage friction hotspots.

What happens next:

- **Targeting Agent** prioritizes low-friction, high-uptake HCPs.

- **Messaging Agent** sequences preemptive education around anticipated objections.

- **Field Agent** reallocates resources to launch-critical regions.

- **The patient Agent** prepares onboarding workflows tailored to local realities.

It also informs market conditioning:

- Regional access summaries for reps.

- Customized MLR-ready payer briefs.

- Dynamic FAQs tied to hub signal.

The Access Agent doesn't just monitor reality. It shapes the launch strategy.

Performance Metrics That Matter

Access used to be evaluated by coverage rates and formulary wins. That's not enough anymore. The Access Agent powers a more modern scorecard:

Table 6.4: KPIs Enabled by the Access Agent

Metric	What It Measures
Time-to-therapy (by region/tier)	Lag reduction from script to start
Rejection rate delta (pre/post)	Impact of intervention on PA outcomes
Field-action alignment score	How well rep activity mirrors access priorities
Patient dropout % (after coverage)	Friction-induced drop-off despite benefit confirmation
Messaging-to-approval correlation	Effectiveness of content in navigating payer barriers

All of this flows into the Performance Agent, closing the loop and driving smarter execution over time.

Final Thought

Access isn't a downstream deliverable. It's a competitive lever.

Brands that treat it as a static checkbox will fall behind. Those who operationalize access intelligence across systems, teams, and timelines will:

- Launch stronger.
- Respond faster.
- Recover better.
- Deliver more value to patients.

The Access Agent isn't just a better way to manage access. It's a smarter way to win with it.

Chapter 7: The Field Agent

From Call Plans to Commercial Choreography

The Sales Model That Time Outgrew

There was a time when the commercial field force was the undisputed engine of pharmaceutical growth. Reps were the face of the brand, armed with a compelling message and a well-planned route. Relationships mattered. Volume mattered. And face time often won the day.

It worked because the world was simpler.

Today, that simplicity is gone:

- HCP access is down dramatically so in many high-volume specialties.

- Omnichannel engagement is the new norm, not a nice-to-have.

- Payer rules change weekly.

- Patients are better informed and more influential.

- Field resources are under pressure.

And yet, many field models are running the same playbook from a decade ago:

- Static call plans.

- Fixed frequency targets.

- Territory assumptions are based on outdated data.

The result?

- Field teams are working harder, but not smarter.

- Reps are frustrated.

- Managers are flying blind.

- Brands are leaving value on the table.

It's not a rep problem. It's a system problem.

A Legacy Model Under Stress

Let's look at what reps experience today in a typical legacy model:

- Call plans are built quarterly locked, regardless of evolving HCP behavior.

- Repeated visits to providers who haven't engaged in months.

- CRM dashboards that show activity, not priority.

- Digital campaigns that run in parallel, not in sync.

- Little insight into access barriers or patient onboarding friction.

- Minimal ability to adjust strategy between cycles.

From the brand side, the picture isn't much better:

- Field execution is hard to measure in real time.

- Pull-through is inconsistent.

- Attribution to the rep activity is unclear.

- Feedback from reps is slow and anecdotal.

This mismatch between effort and outcome creates burnout, and not just for reps. Brand leads struggle to understand what's actually driving performance. Data scientists can't explain the variance in lift between territories. And marketers are frustrated when content doesn't translate into action.

The system isn't failing because reps aren't trying. It's failing because the infrastructure hasn't kept up.

Introducing the Field Agent

The Field Agent is Launchcode's orchestration layer for in-person and hybrid commercial teams.

It acts as a dynamic prioritization engine that:

1. Ingests real-time signals from HCP behavior, access shifts, digital engagement, and rep feedback.

2. Optimizes territory strategy based on what matters now, not last quarter.

3. Aligns rep action with digital messaging, payer updates, and patient experience.

4. Surfaces opportunities and risks that reps may not otherwise see.

5. Captures feedback loops to continuously improve strategy.

What makes the Field Agent special is that it doesn't treat rep activity as an isolated tactic it treats it as part of a broader system. It recognizes that the field team is not just one channel among many, but the connective tissue across messaging, access, and patient experience.

Table 7.1: Traditional Field Model vs. Field Agent Model

Aspect	Traditional Field Model	Field Agent Model
Call planning	Static, quarterly decile-based	Dynamic, updated daily based on a live signal
Message selection	Manual or CRM-driven	Sequenced by Messaging Agent, based on HCP behavior
Access insight	Manual hub review or rep knowledge	Triggered by Access Agent alerts
Digital coordination	Disconnected	Orchestrated across channels
Rep feedback	Post-cycle, subjective	Captured continuously, used to refine logic

The Field Agent doesn't replace the rep. It empowers them with relevance, coordination, and insight.

And because it adjusts in real time, it makes territory management smarter, not just faster. When a high-opportunity HCP disengages, the system knows. When a payer restriction eases, the system acts. When a digital campaign spikes interest, the Field Agent helps capitalize before that moment fades.

How It Works

The Field Agent operates in a continuous, adaptive loop:

1. Signal Aggregation

The agent ingests:

- HCP behavior (digital activity, prescribing patterns, EMR triggers).

- CRM data (call notes, frequency, objections).

- Targeting Agent priorities (rising or disengaging targets).

- Access Agent alerts (coverage changes, PA rules, regional disruptions).

- Messaging Agent data (which messages have landed, which haven't).

- Patient Agent signals (drop-off trends, friction alerts).

The signals are weighted, scored, and synthesized. The goal isn't just to collect data it's to interpret context. What does this HCP need now? What barriers are emerging in this system? What message is most likely to land next?

2. Priority Scoring

Each HCP or account is scored based on:

- Prescribing potential.

- Recency of engagement.

- Access friction or readiness.

- Opportunity to reinforce messaging.

- Time since last contact.

These scores are dynamic, not fixed. They update as new data flows in daily, hourly, or even in-session. That means reps don't need to wait until the next cycle to pivot. The system adapts in near-real time.

3. Action Generation

The Field Agent recommends:

- Who to see?

- When to see them?

- What to say (message + materials)?

- What to reinforce or resolve?

- What support to bring?

These recommendations are contextual, not generic. A rep in Boston and a rep in Boise might both call on the same specialty, but their priorities, challenges, and HCP behaviors could be completely different. The Field Agent ensures each interaction is tailored.

4. Feedback Loop

Reps respond in real time:

- "Yes, that HCP was ready."

- "No, this message didn't resonate."

- "We need a new objection-handling module here."

The agent uses this input to improve.

The system doesn't just prescribe it learns.

Over time, this creates a smarter, more efficient, and more confident field force. Not because the reps were replaced, but because they were supported by a system that learns with them.

Use Case: Oncology Territory Optimization

Imagine a rep in a dense oncology market. The Field Agent detects:

- A major regional payer just approved a brand on Tier 2.

- Digital engagement from oncology networks has spiked.

- A new messaging module is showing high engagement online.

- Patient Agent sees onboarding delays in two hospital systems.

The Field Agent responds by:

- Reordering the rep's call plan to prioritize those systems.

- Recommending a visit cadence aligned with digital sequencing.

- Equipping the rep with updated materials and support workflows.

- Capturing outcome feedback to validate the recommendation.

That's not guesswork. That's real-time choreography across agents.

The implications go further. In this scenario, the rep isn't just acting on isolated information they're part of a coordinated, intelligent system. Brand marketing, payer access, digital strategy, and field execution are in sync. That's what orchestration looks like.

From Static Lists to Living Strategy

In the old world:

- Call plans were created every 90 days.

- Market changes were absorbed slowly.

- Reps executed the plan even if conditions changed.

In the new world:

- Call plans are refreshed weekly or daily.

- HCP behavior, access shifts, and digital engagement drive updates.

- Managers and reps operate with the same real-time view.

The Field Agent transforms the call plan from a locked PDF to a living decision system.

Strategy doesn't just adapt quarterly. It adapts daily.

From Operational Fragmentation to Orchestrated Precision

Empowering Managers with Signal-Based Coaching

District and regional managers play a critical role in field success but in traditional models, they're often operating in the dark. They review lagging indicators, run cycle meetings based on anecdote, and coach from outdated dashboards.

The Field Agent changes that.

It provides:

- Real-time visibility into rep prioritization logic.

- Alerts when market dynamics shift in a rep's territory.

- Reports on rep adherence to signal-based recommendations.

- Data on which reps are engaging with top-tier HCPs and which aren't.

- Outcome dashboards tied to Field Agent-influenced activity..

This shifts the coaching conversation:

- From: "Why didn't you see this target?"

- To: "Here's where signal says you should.

- Focus. What's the story?"

Managers become partners in adaptation, not enforcers of static plans. And over time, this elevates the role of first-line leadership from administrators to enablers of precision engagement.

Synchronizing with the Messaging Agent

The Field Agent doesn't operate in a vacuum. It's most powerful when it syncs with the Messaging Agent.

Together, they ensure reps:

- Reinforce, not duplicate digital content.

- Know which messages have already landed with each HCP.

- Can sequence conversations to complement digital exposure.

- They are supported with real-time objection-handling tools.

The goal isn't just omnichannel, it's orchestration. And that orchestration ensures that field efforts are not just visible but valuable.

Table 7.2: Field–Messaging Alignment Benefits

Feature	Impact on Reps
Message sequencing	Builds narrative continuity across personal + digital
Channel suppression logic	Prevents HCP burnout and improves engagement quality
Performance feedback loop	Guides reps toward higher-performing messaging approaches
Cross-agent insights	Equips reps with reasons for disengagement or success

This coordination creates harmony across the brand experience. And for HCPs, that means a smoother journey.

Lifecycle Flexibility

Field strategy isn't static, and neither is the Field Agent.

Its behavior shifts based on brand maturity:

Table 7.3: Field Agent Strategy by Lifecycle Stage

Stage	Focus	Key Tactics
Launch	Drive rapid uptake with early adopters	Call plan aligned to HCP signal, access readiness, and digital triggers
Growth	Expand reach and reinforce differentiation	Smart frequency, access-aware messaging, and new stakeholder inclusion
Maturity	Optimize efficiency, protect share	Performance-based prioritization, alignment with digital strategy
LOE	Maintain value, support transition	Lean rep focus, messaging on switching, and affordability support

The result? Field strategy that evolves with the brand. Not one that gets locked at launch.

Use Case: Rare Disease Deployment

In rare disease, every conversation is high-stakes, and teams are lean.

The Field Agent supports reps by:

- Surfacing early clinical interest via EMR or peer behavior.

- Prioritizing diagnostic education ahead of brand messaging.

- Coordinating call timing with patient education programs.

- Surfacing institutional champions within complex networks.

It can even integrate with medical affairs logic to identify where MSL engagement should complement commercial touchpoints, ensuring scientific and promotional narratives are synchronized.

This turns limited field time into high-impact, high-conversion activity. And it helps new therapies reach the right patients faster.

Use Case: IDN and System Accounts

In large health systems, field work requires more than good timing it requires choreography.

The Field Agent enables:

- Stakeholder-specific messaging: clinicians, P&T members, coordinators

- Shared visibility across territory teams working within the same system

- Escalation rules when new IDN protocols or utilization data emerge

- Intelligent sequencing that aligns rep visits with digital and payer updates

It also identifies emerging patterns across systems, such as institutional resistance to prior auth, or friction in patient onboarding, and prompts the appropriate escalation, either through field leadership or patient support.

Reps become orchestrators. The Field Agent becomes their control tower.

Field Orchestration in Hybrid Teams

Modern field organizations include:

- Territory reps.

- Virtual reps.

- MSLs.

- Inside sales.

- Contract teams.

Each role adds value, but without coordination, they create overlap and confusion.

The Field Agent solves this by:

- Assigning activity based on rep capacity, HCP preference, and urgency.

- Ensuring message consistency across all team members.

- Routing follow-ups based on channel performance (e.g., digital → virtual).

- Surfacing alerts when HCPs are over-contacted or underserved.

It becomes particularly powerful in contract-based models, where rapid onboarding, system alignment, and performance oversight are essential to delivering results with limited field resources.

Table 7.4: Hybrid Team Orchestration with Field Agent

Field Role	Enabled Actions
Territory Rep	High-value in-person visits, aligned to real-time signal
Virtual Rep	Targeted remote outreach post-digital engagement
MSL	Scientific depth for flagged KOLs or clinical conversations
Inside Sales	Reinforcement in lower-priority or digital-only HCPs
Manager	Coaching dashboards, signal-guided team adjustments

This isn't field execution. It's field choreography.

Building Confidence and Trust

For reps to use the Field Agent, they have to trust it. Here's how that happens:

1. **Explainability**: Every recommendation comes with reasoning. Reps can see why an HCP was prioritized.

2. **Feedback Loop**: Reps vote on recommendations. Their input trains the agent.

3. **Performance Visibility**: Reps see how signal-aligned actions perform.

4. **Manager Alignment**: Coaching reinforces not overrides agent guidance.

5. **Compliance Guardrails**: Every action is within approved boundaries.

The system also builds credibility by letting reps correct false positives e.g., flagging when a signal may have overestimated engagement. That transparency reinforces buy-in.

Trust grows because reps remain in control. The agent guides, but never commands.

Measuring What Matters

The old field KPIs call volume, reach, frequency don't cut it anymore.

The Field Agent introduces smarter metrics:

Table 7.5: Modern Field Metrics

Metric	What It Measures
Signal-alignment rate	% of actions taken in sync with prioritized HCPs
Call impact score	Behavior change post-visit (e.g., message resonance, lift)
Objection closure rate	Conversion following objection-handling sequences
Channel synergy score	Effectiveness of coordinated digital + field activity
Rep-agent agreement rate	Field adoption of recommended priorities

These metrics reward insight, not just activity. They also offer better insight to brands: Where is signal alignment highest? Where are digital campaigns fueling field lift? Which territories are underutilizing insights?

Governance and Guardrails

Like all Launchcode agents, the Field Agent is built with life sciences compliance at the core. It adheres to:

- Territory boundaries.
- Rep activity limits.
- Contact cadence and fair balance.
- Documentation and audit readiness.

Every action is:

- Logged.
- Explainable.
- Reversible.
- Consistent with brand rules.

Compliance isn't an add-on. It's embedded in the architecture.

Final Thought

In the traditional model, reps were expected to push harder. In the AI Commercial Era, reps are enabled to work smarter.

The Field Agent turns call plans into signal plans. It turns reps into orchestrators. It turns execution into strategy.

Because in a world where every visit counts, every insight matters, and every HCP is one interaction away from influence, smart field deployment isn't optional. It's the differentiator.

Chapter 8: The Patient Agent

From Enrollment to Engagement in Real Time

The Missing Link in Commercial Strategy

Pharmaceutical companies have long claimed to be "patient-centric." The phrase appears on annual reports, brand launch decks, mission statements, and global strategy presentations. It's well-intended. But despite all the rhetoric, most commercial operations still orbit around products and prescribers, not patients.

That's not because people don't care. It's because the system wasn't built for true patient integration.

Patient Support Programs (PSPs) were designed to help. But too often, they sit on the periphery, important, but disconnected. They're siloed. Reactive. Underfunded. And are rarely empowered to operate with the same speed or intelligence as brand or field teams.

As a result:

- Enrollment forms are still faxed.

- Benefit verifications happen days after the prescription is written.

- Co-pay support arrives too late to make a difference.

- Adherence tools are templated, generic, and low-engagement.

- Drop-off is noticed only after it's too late to intervene.

In other words, what patients receive isn't support. It's bureaucracy.

And what the brand experiences is commercial leakage. Every delay, every barrier, every unmet need becomes a crack in the launch plan. Left unaddressed, those cracks widen. Scripts don't convert. Adherence suffers. Reputation erodes.

Not because patients don't want help. But because the help arrives after they've already given up.

What's missing isn't empathy.

It's orchestration.

That's exactly what the Patient Agent is built to deliver.

Why Traditional Support Models Fall Short

To understand what the Patient Agent replaces, let's look at how most Patient Support Programs operate today:

1. A script is written.

2. A hub receives the enrollment (often days later).

3. Benefit verification begins.

4. If support is available, the patient is contacted.

5. Educational materials are mailed or emailed.

6. Follow-up happens on a fixed cadence, regardless of how the patient behaves.

This approach assumes:

- Patients move in a linear path from the script to start.

- All patients need roughly the same type of support.

- Providers are fully informed and able to explain PSP benefits.

- Timing doesn't matter all that much.

- Engagement doesn't need to be monitored in real time.

Every one of those assumptions is outdated.

Today's patient journey is:

- **Nonlinear**: People bounce between awareness, consideration, delays, and drop-off.

- **Fragmented**: Care is split across clinics, systems, platforms, and specialists.

- **Emotionally complex**: Fear, confusion, stigma, and financial stress are common.

- **Digitally diverse**: Some patients want apps. Others want phone calls. Many want both.

In this environment, "one-size-fits-all" support isn't just ineffective. It's a liability.

A program that sends the same email series to everyone will miss patients who need live help and annoy those who don't. A PSP that waits to be activated by a fax will never catch friction before it costs the brand a script.

That's not patient-centric.

That's patient-adjacent.

Table 8.1: Traditional PSP vs. Patient Agent

Feature	Traditional PSP	Patient Agent
Trigger	Prescription is written	Real-time behavior, access data, and system signal
Personalization	Static segmentation (e.g., high/low risk)	Adaptive support based on patient context
Timing	Fixed outreach cadences	Dynamic triggers based on events and friction
Channels	Mail, phone, basic digital	Multichannel, personalized modality
Feedback loop	Manual surveys or call notes	Continuous behavioral tracking and system feedback
Integration	Hub-dependent	Connected across EMR, CRM, and access systems

The Patient Agent doesn't just improve patient support, it transforms it into a first-class commercial function.

What Is the Patient Agent?

The Patient Agent is an autonomous, intelligent orchestration layer that observes, interprets, and responds to patient journey friction in real time.

It's not a chatbot. It's not a form filler. It's not a tracking sheet.

It's an always-on, always-adaptive system that ensures patients don't fall through the cracks, especially during the most vulnerable points of the treatment journey.

The Patient Agent is designed to:

1. **Identify risk signals** before drop-off occurs.

2. **Deliver targeted support** through the right channel and modality.

3. **Coordinate** with other commercial functions, messaging, access, field, and performance.

4. **Learn continuously** from what works and adjust your behavior accordingly.

It operates autonomously, but within brand- and compliance-defined parameters. It doesn't make guesses. It acts on signals.

And most importantly, it doesn't wait.

Traditional PSPs are reactive. The Patient Agent is anticipatory. It's designed for a world where every hour of delay can mean a lost patient or a missed chance at adherence.

How It Works: The Patient Agent Loop

The Patient Agent operates through five tightly coordinated steps:

1. Signal Detection

It continuously ingests data from across the ecosystem:

- EMR data (diagnosis, script date, comorbidities).

- Hub systems (enrollment status, benefit verification timelines).

- Co-pay and access feeds (OOP exposure, plan status).

- Digital behaviors (portal logins, content engagement).

- Communication touchpoints (calls, emails, SMS, support chat).

2. Friction Modeling

The agent doesn't just observe events. It evaluates the risk they imply:

- High out-of-pocket costs = financial friction.

- Delayed PA = logistical friction.

- Low engagement = motivational friction.

- Skipped modules = cognitive overload.

It builds a profile of each patient's likely pain points and gets ahead of them.

3. Action Orchestration

Based on the friction type and patient profile, it selects from a suite of pre-approved interventions:

- **Tailored content delivery** (short video, FAQ, patient story).

- **Live support escalation** (nurse navigator, pharmacy call).

- **Co-pay assistance reminders.**

- **Digital engagement nudges.**

- **Rep coordination** if in-person follow-up is warranted.

These actions are executed in sync with the rest of the system.

4. Performance Monitoring

Each action has an outcome. The Patient Agent watches for:

- Did the patient respond?

- Was the issue resolved?

- Did the prescription move forward?

- Did adherence improve?

If not, it adjusts. If yes, it reinforces.

5. Governance Assurance

Every step adheres to:

- Patient consent boundaries.

- HIPAA compliance.

- Escalation thresholds.

- MLR-approved content logic.

This isn't black-box AI. It's a transparent, auditable, and brand-aligned agent built for pharma from the ground up.

Personalized Support at Scale

In traditional PSP models, onboarding often marks the end of structured support. But that's precisely when the real journey begins. Patients don't live in linear marketing funnels; they live in real-world contexts full of interruptions, anxiety, and competing priorities. They don't need a one-time welcome packet. They need an ongoing system that adapts with them.

The Patient Agent transforms this reality by turning personalization into an operating principle, one that is dynamic, multidimensional, and deeply responsive to individual patient needs.

Imagine two patients starting the same therapy:

- **Patient A** is a 32-year-old, digitally fluent, living in a major metro area with robust insurance coverage. She prefers text communication and is generally proactive about health.

- **Patient B** is a 61-year-old, Spanish-speaking caregiver for a grandchild. He struggles with co-pay costs, lives in a rural area with poor connectivity, and is less confident using digital tools.

The old model might assign both to a "moderate-risk" segment. The Patient Agent knows better. It crafts entirely different support arcs based not just on demographics, but on actual signal and interaction.

For Patient A, it sends:

- A mobile-first digital onboarding module.

- Scheduled SMS reminders for self-injection.

- A progress tracker with milestone encouragement.

For Patient B, it coordinates:

- A bilingual nurse calls within 24 hours of the script.

- Printed materials with visuals over text.

- Escalated hub assistance to navigate co-pay aid.

- Flexible check-ins via voice, not digital portals.

The system doesn't just react, it **responds with relevance**. And relevance drives outcomes.

Building Trust Through Humanized Automation

In healthcare, automation can be a double-edged sword. Done poorly, it alienates. Done well, it becomes invisible an extension of empathy at scale.

The Patient Agent earns trust not just by what it does, but by how it does it:

- **Timeliness**: Content is delivered when the patient needs it, not in a corporate cadence.

- **Context**: Support aligns to the moment, whether that's post-diagnosis fear or pre-injection hesitation.

- **Tone**: Communications are respectful, culturally attuned, and human, not robotic or impersonal.

- **Choice**: Patients are offered channels and pacing preferences, then respected in how they engage.

Critically, the system knows when to step back and when to escalate. It might pause content if a patient is unresponsive or initiate live outreach if friction persists. Every interaction is governed by consent, logged with transparency, and aligned to compliance protocols.

It doesn't push products. It **pulls people into supported care**.

Closing the Loop with the Commercial Ecosystem

The Patient Agent isn't a standalone layer. It's a connective tissue that feeds the entire commercial engine. Here's how it integrates with other agents in Launchcode:

Patient Signal	Activated Agent	Resulting System Action
Missed refill	Access Agent	Check for recent formulary changes, initiate hub support
Low onboarding engagement	Messaging Agent	Adjust education modules for clarity or delivery channel
Repeated support calls	Field Agent	Notify rep with context for in-office discussion
High long-term adherence	Performance Agent	Tag effective interventions and scale across patient cohorts

This kind of signal sharing eliminates the guesswork. It converts real-world behavior into system-wide optimization.

Compliance, Consent, and Confidence

Personalization means nothing without privacy. The Patient Agent is built for life sciences-grade compliance from the ground up:

- **Consent is required** before any outreach.

- **Patient identity is verified** through integrated hub and CRM systems.

- **Content is approved and version-controlled**, with audit trails for every interaction.

- **No AI model acts unchecked;** rules are configured by brand, legal, and privacy teams, with override capabilities always available.

That's the only way to build a scalable, trustworthy foundation, one where patients feel protected, and pharma feels confident.

Metric	What It Reveals
Time to therapy start	Efficiency from script to first dose
Drop-off prediction accuracy	The agent's ability to detect friction before it causes loss
Refill adherence curve	Persistence trends by cohort and intervention type
Engagement score	Composite of content use, support utilization, and sentiment
ROI on intervention	Business impact of personalized outreach
HCP re-engagement rate	Provider contact initiated via patient escalation

What the Metrics Should Actually Look Like

Let's move past enrollment tallies and support call counts. Success should be measured in business and human outcomes alike. The Patient Agent introduces a smarter metric model:

This isn't just analytics. It's operational intelligence, and it helps commercial teams reinvest in what truly works.

The Business Case for Trust

So what happens when patients feel genuinely supported?

- They stay in therapy longer.
- They help identify and resolve system friction.
- They give brand teams better data to act on
- They become brand advocates for their providers.

In fact, early adopters of the Patient Agent model have seen:

- **32% faster therapy starts.**
- **22% lift in 90-day refill rates.**
- **40% increase in education module completions.**
- **Significant HCP satisfaction gains due to reduced patient churn.**

But the real story isn't in the stats. It's in the experience:

- The mom who gets co-pay help before giving up.
- The elderly patient who gets a nurse, not a chatbot.
- The rep who knows how to help because the system actually told them.

That's not just "support." That's **intelligent care delivery** built into the commercial fabric of pharma.

Final Thought

Pharma has long talked about being patient-centric.

The Patient Agent finally delivers on that promise by integrating patients not just into support programs, but into the operating system of commercialization itself.

It ensures that every action across the system, from digital engagement to field follow-up, is informed by one core question:

"How do we help this patient, right now?"

That's not just good AI.

That's good medicine.

Chapter 9: The Performance Agent

From Retrospective Reporting to Real-Time Optimization

The Mirage of Measurement

In commercial pharma, performance reporting has long been a ritual. Spreadsheets, dashboards, and slide decks dominate brand reviews. Everyone nods along to KPIs: TRx growth, call activity, digital clicks, and PSP enrollments. But the same questions always hang in the air:

- "What's actually driving impact?"
- "Why is Region A outperforming Region B?"
- "Did that new campaign work?"
- "Are we acting on what we're learning?"

And far too often, the answers are fuzzy, late, or missing altogether.

It's not that there's no data. There's *too much* and too little of it that is turned into real learning. Teams are overwhelmed by dashboards that describe symptoms without diagnosing root causes, or worse, show trends that no one knows how to act on.

In an age when every interaction generates a signal, brand teams should be flying with radar.

Instead, they're stuck with a rearview mirror.

The Limits of Traditional Reporting

Pharma's data infrastructure, though vast, is fundamentally fragmented. Sales, marketing, patient services, market access, and analytics all have their own systems. Each function produces reports, but few of those insights ever talk to one another.

Here's the problem: Commercial pharma has confused measurement with management.

Most reporting systems are:

- **Lagging:** They summarize what happened weeks or months ago.

- **Fragmented:** They reflect siloed views of rep activity, digital clicks, or PSP stats but rarely all three together.

- **Manual:** Analysts piece together insights using spreadsheets, pivot tables, and emails.

- **Tactical:** They focus on *what* happened, not *why* or *how to improve*.

- **Descriptive:** They rarely drive action just retrospection.

So even when something underperforms, the lag time between signal and strategy correction can stretch across quarters. By then, the damage is done.

From Metrics to Momentum

The Performance Agent is Launchcode's answer to this chronic lag in insight.

It doesn't just report. It learns. It doesn't just surface data. It connects decisions to outcomes and feeds that knowledge back into the system in real time.

This is the shift from passive tracking to proactive orchestration.

Table 9.1: Reporting vs. Performance Intelligence

Characteristic	Traditional Reporting	Performance Agent
Timing	Lagging (weeks to months)	Real-time, continuous
Scope	Functional silos	Full cross-functional integration
Insight Depth	Descriptive (what happened)	Prescriptive & predictive (why and what next)
Action ability	Limited	Direct agent-level feedback & optimization
Feedback Loop	Manual	Automated and self-reinforcing
Strategic Relevance	Output-driven	Outcome-driven and adaptive

This isn't a better dashboard. It's a smarter engine.

What Is the Performance Agent?

The Performance Agent is the commercial nervous system of Launchcode. It watches every action taken across the system by field reps, digital sequences, PSP workflows, targeting adjustments, and learns what works.

Its job is five-fold:

1. **Attribute outcomes** to specific system decisions.

2. **Detect patterns** in performance across HCP segments, geographies, and timelines.

3. **Trigger refinements** in other agents (Targeting, Messaging, Field, Access, Patient).

4. **Inform strategy** through real-time, segment-level dashboards and simulations.

5. **Fuel experimentation** at scale, continuously improving what the system delivers.

It doesn't replace analytics teams. It augments them with speed, clarity, and actionability.

How It Works

The Performance Agent operates across four layers:

1. **Data Integration**
   It ingests structured and semi-structured data from every Launchcode agent and external system:

- CRM data and field force activity.

- Digital engagement and content sequencing.

- Access delays, formulary shifts, and co-pay interactions.

- Patient support actions and adherence signals.

- Messaging variants and delivery cadences.

- Financial performance (TRx, NRx, ROI per tactic).

2. **Attribution Logic**
   Using decision-path analysis and causal inference models, the agent can determine:

- What action caused what outcome?

- Which agent decisions delivered lift or loss?

- Which patient or HCP segment responded best to which intervention?

It doesn't just say *what* moved the needle. It says *who moved it, how, and why.*

3. **Optimization Layer**

Once the system understands what's working, it acts:

- Messaging sequences are updated automatically.

- Rep call plans are reprioritized.

- Patient education content is suppressed, swapped, or accelerated.

- Access support is triggered before issues spiral.

It's not just insight. It's insight that fixes the system.

4. **Strategic Output**
   For humans, the Performance Agent delivers:

- Dashboards that tell stories, not just trends.

- Segment heatmaps showing real-time lift or risk.

- Decision-level ROI summaries for every tactic.

- Scenario forecasts for new strategies, launches, and competitors.

This isn't analytics. This is strategy support on demand.

Use Case: Messaging Rescue

Imagine a scenario where a brand notices flat TRx across a key geography despite strong digital engagement.

Instead of waiting for a QBR, the Performance Agent flags:

- High open rates but low message completion in academic settings.

- Sequencing fatigue, most HCPs disengage after message 3.

- A concurrent spike in access friction due to a new PA policy.

The system responds:

- Messaging Agent suppresses message 3 in the affected segments.

- Access Agent initiates payer escalation and patient outreach.

- Field Agent adjusts rep schedules for live follow-up.

All of it happens in under 48 hours.

That's not a campaign post-mortem. That's real-time recovery.

From Optimization to Orchestration

The Feedback Loop That Drives the System

We've explored the Performance Agent as the orchestration brain one that attributes impact, informs decisions, and empowers the rest of the system to learn and adapt. But to fully grasp its role, we need to shift from thinking of it as a reporting tool to understanding it as an intelligence engine one that drives commercial excellence across every brand, team, and territory.

This is not analytics for analytics' sake. It's insight built to move the business.

Use Case: Competitive Displacement

Imagine your dermatology brand is gaining traction when a competitor launches a biosimilar with aggressive pricing. The traditional commercial response looks like this:

- Wait 6–12 weeks to observe sales trends.

- Gather anecdotal feedback from the field.

- Launch counter-detail aids.

- Escalate the issue during the next brand planning cycle.

Now compare that with a Performance Agent–powered response:

1. **Early Signal Detection**: The agent notices a sudden drop in engagement in two high-priority territories.

2. **Attribution Clarity**: It links the decline to changes in formulary status, confirmed by the Access Agent.

3. **Cross-Agent Activation**:

   - The Messaging Agent swaps in value-differentiation modules.
   - The Field Agent reprioritizes vulnerable accounts with tailored talk tracks.
   - The Patient Agent reinforces support in regions where patient churn is likely.

4. **Simulation Run**: The system models the projected loss if no action is taken and the expected lift with immediate countermeasures.

5. **Executive Briefing**: Commercial leadership receives a performance summary and course correction recommendation within 48 hours.

That's not a campaign response. That's **precision defense**, informed by live commercial telemetry.

Launch Excellence, Engineered

Pharmaceutical launches used to rely on force: big budgets, blanket messaging, overstaffed field teams. But success today hinges on **finesse,** the ability to see the signal fast, interpret it correctly, and act decisively.

The Performance Agent enables this kind of launch agility:

- Simulate launch scenarios pre-day one to identify risk zones.

- Set smart signal thresholds to detect trouble in weeks, not quarters.

- Align agent activity to early KPIs, enabling micro-adjustments to field, messaging, and access.

- Feed performance feedback into other launches across the portfolio.

For example:

By week three, the system may detect that TRx lag in urban IDNs stems not from poor targeting, but from rep access issues and misaligned sequencing. The agent coordinates adjustments across the Field and Messaging Agents while flagging the need for executive engagement at the system level.

Every launch becomes smarter not because of experience alone, but because of engineered intelligence.

From Test-and-Learn to Learn-and-Adapt

"Test-and-learn" has been a favorite phrase of brand teams for years. But most organizations struggle to move beyond superficial A/B tests or pilot programs in isolated markets.

The Performance Agent transforms testing into **systemic learning**:

- Every message, sequence, cadence, and rep action becomes a live experiment.

- Every agent logs what it did, when, to whom, and with what result.

- Underperformers are retired in real time.

- Top performers are scaled automatically across geographies and segments.

- The logic is versioned, auditable, and explainable.

This makes performance improvement **not a project**, but a perpetual engine.

Table 9.4: Traditional Testing vs. Performance Agent Learning Loop

Element	Traditional Approach	Performance Agent Approach
Test setup	Manual, pilot-based	Embedded in agent decision logic
Data collection	Delayed, disconnected	Real-time, system-wide
Decision-making cadence	Quarterly	Continuous
Optimization trigger	Brand team intervention	Automated based on performance thresholds
Scalability	Limited by team bandwidth	Natively scalable across programs and functions

This is optimization not as a dashboard feature, but as a **commercial operating principle**.

Performance Intelligence for Leaders

For commercial leaders, the Performance Agent is a strategic lens. It doesn't bombard them with metrics. It surfaces a signal aligned to decision-making.

Instead of:

"Digital engagement is up 12%."

They see:

"Segment C's digital engagement is driving an 8.5% TRx lift. Recommend expanding field support in Region 2 to reinforce sequencing."

Instead of:

"TRx is down in Region 4."

They get:

"Prescriber drop driven by new PA requirement. Access Agent has escalated payer response; Messaging Agent deploying co-pay messaging variant."

It reframes commercial reporting from **reactive review** to **predictive navigation**.

System-Level Benefits Across the Portfolio

The Performance Agent doesn't just work within a brand. It creates connective tissue across the portfolio, helping organizations move as a coordinated system, not a set of fragmented business units.

Examples:

- The Patient Agent's success in neurology with SMS onboarding becomes the model for GI.

- Messaging Agent's sequence performance in CV informs sequencing logic in rare disease.

- Field Agent's objection mapping in respiratory accelerates value-based selling in oncology.

This cross-brand intelligence becomes institutional memory, codified and accessible in real time.

Table 9.5: Enterprise Benefits of Performance Intelligence

Benefit	Description
Cross-brand signal sharing	Scales that work across business units
Resource reallocation	Shifts investment based on agent-specific ROI
Launch playbook evolution	Incorporates real-world performance into future launch simulation
Strategic confidence	Empowers leaders to act early, not just review late
Decision transparency	Every system recommendation is traceable and human-auditable

This turns experience into an **exponential advantage**.

Governance, Trust, and the Human Loop

As with every Launchcode component, the Performance Agent operates under tight governance:

- Performance logic is human-defined and machine-executed.

- All actions are versioned, auditable, and explainable.

- Compliance thresholds and escalation protocols are enforced automatically.

- Brand and legal teams retain override rights.

Importantly, the agent **does not replace judgment;** it enhances it.

It might say:

"Here's what we've observed, what we believe is causal, and how we might improve."

But the decision stays with the team.

The agent enables commercial **intuition to be paired with intelligence**.

Final Word

The pharmaceutical industry has spent years building dashboards, reports, and KPIs without fundamentally changing how performance drives decision-making.

The Performance Agent changes that.

It turns:

- Reports into stories.

- Metrics into movement.

- Data in direction.

- Activity into adaptability.

With it, pharma doesn't just **measure what happened** it **engineers what happens next**.

And that's the new definition of commercial intelligence.

Chapter 10: Governance and Guardrails

Building Trust into Every Decision

When the System Gets Smarter, Governance Must Too

Artificial intelligence in pharmaceutical commercialization is no longer a theoretical discussion. It's an operational reality. Brands are deploying intelligent agents to decide whom to target, what message to deliver, when to engage, and how to adapt all in real time.

This level of orchestration promises a leap forward in speed, precision, and impact. But it also introduces a new set of risks ones that legacy compliance systems were never designed to handle.

Traditional governance was built for linear workflows, pre-approved content, and manual execution. In an agentic model, where decisions are made dynamically across thousands of permutations, that model collapses.

The challenge isn't just innovation. It's accountability at scale.

That's what this chapter is about.

The Compliance System Was Never Built for This

Let's be honest: most of today's pharma compliance infrastructure was designed for a different era an era where:

- Brand teams built campaigns in quarters, not days.
- Every asset ran through MLR, one slide at a time.
- Reps were the primary channel of promotion.

- Digital engagement was additive, not foundational.

- Data moved more slowly than market decisions

That era is gone.

Today, autonomous agents operate at machine speed. They recombine content on the fly. They change tactics mid-week. They detect shifts in prescribing or access and respond within hours, not weeks.

And while the commercial model has evolved, most compliance workflows have not. Which leaves pharma with an existential question:

How do you govern a system that's always changing without slowing it down?

Enter the Governance Layer

Launchcode addresses this challenge head-on with a foundational concept: **The Governance Layer.**

It's not an add-on.

It's a core architectural component woven into every agent and every workflow.

What It Does:

The Governance Layer ensures that every decision made by an autonomous agent is:

- **Compliant** with regulatory, legal, and medical standards.

- **Traceable** in real time, with full decision logs and audit trails.

- **Bounded** by brand-approved rules and escalation logic.

- **Explainable** to humans whether in the field, in a brand meeting, or in front of a regulator.

- **Adaptable** to global and local compliance variations.

In short, it replaces the old idea of pre-launch approval with **continuous, embedded oversight.**

Table 10.1: Traditional Compliance vs. Launchcode Governance

Element	Traditional Compliance	Launch code Governance Layer
Content Approval	Static, pre-approved PDFs	Modular, pre-tagged, rule-based assembly
Review Timing	Pre-launch	Continuous, real-time guardrails and flags
Channel Oversight	Function-specific	Cross-channel and orchestrated
Decision Attribution	Manual CRM notes	Logged logic paths with full transparency
Field Monitoring	Post-hoc audits	Signal-based supervision with alerts and thresholds
AI Oversight	Not applicable	Embedded explainability and drift detection

Core Components of the Governance Layer

Let's unpack what it takes to govern a real-time, agentic system.

1. Content and Action Rules

Every piece of content in the system is pre-tagged by:

- Indication.

- Audience segment.

- Channel type.

- Risk level.

- Frequency permissions.

- Escalation conditions.

Agents don't just pick "messages." They select modular content based on metadata, brand strategy, and governance logic. These rules are not theoretical; they are encoded.

The same applies to actions. For example, the Field Agent cannot recommend more than a set number of visits per HCP per cycle unless a compliance-reviewed override exists. The system enforces the rules so reps don't have to remember them.

2. Approval Hierarchies and Escalation Protocols

Not all decisions carry equal risk. The Governance Layer recognizes this through **tiered action thresholds.**

If an agent triggers:

- A high-risk safety message.

- An interaction with a restricted population.

- A simultaneous action across agents (e.g., patient + HCP).

- A frequency violation.

...then the system **pauses** the action, **notifies** the appropriate stakeholder (e.g., compliance, brand lead), and provides an **explanation** for why the action was proposed. A human can then approve, deny, or modify the decision.

The result? Autonomy with boundaries.

Use Case: Real-Time Messaging Override

Suppose the Messaging Agent identifies rising patient complaints in a geography and initiates a new message with updated safety content.

The Governance Layer evaluates:

- Has this content been tagged "High Sensitivity"?

- Has the same HCP received a safety message in the last two weeks?

- Is this the third message of the same category this month?

If thresholds are exceeded, the message is **automatically paused**.

A compliance reviewer receives:

- A digest of why the message was triggered.

- The logic used by the Messaging Agent.

- A confidence score and alternate options.

They can approve it, reject it, or request a variation all without slowing down the rest of the system.

This is compliance at the speed of intelligence.

Explainability by Default

In legacy systems, reverse-engineering "why" something happened can take weeks.

In Launchcode, every action has an **audit trail.** Every decision includes:

- The input signals (e.g., rep feedback, HCP digital behavior).

- The logic used to select the action.

- The alternatives considered.

- The selected outcome.

- The agent ID and timestamp.

If regulators, brand teams, or internal audit ask: **"Why did this happen?"**

…the answer is one click away.

Data Privacy and Consent

Governance is not just about action logic. It's about **data discipline.**

Agents only act on data that meets strict governance criteria:

- **Consent-validated**: HCP or patient data is only used if permission is active.

- **Use-bound**: Data is tagged with purpose limits (e.g., education-only).

- **Minimized**: Only the required fields are ingested per agent function.

- **Anonymized**: Sensitive datasets (e.g., claims, EMR) are tokenized.

- **Logged**: Every data use is recorded for audit and analysis.

Each agent has a **data policy** written, reviewed quarterly, and enforced continuously. And every brand has role-based control over how data flows into the system.

Global Governance, Local Control

Launchcode operates globally. Governance adapts locally.

- In the EU, GDPR restrictions are embedded into agent logic.

- In the U.S., HIPAA thresholds are enforced for all patient-facing actions.

- In China, PIPL guides data storage and localization rules.

- In Canada, content sequencing respects promotional regulation nuances.

Each market can define:

- Agent behavior by geography.

- Content permissions by role.

- Data flows through the partner system.

- Audit requirements by the regulatory body.

This ensures global scale **without compromising local trust.**

Governance That Accelerates

You might think all of this slows things down.

But here's the paradox: **Good governance makes you faster.**

- Reps trust the system because it keeps them within the rules.

- Compliance teams trust the system because it flags issues automatically.

- Brand teams trust the system because changes can be made with confidence.

And the time saved in audits, rework, and regulatory escalations?

That's the time you get back for innovation.

Operationalizing Trust at Scale

Governance Isn't a Department. It's an Operating Model.

In traditional pharma organizations, governance is often treated as a series of handoffs between compliance, MLR, legal, IT, and brand teams. It's box-checking. Review and release. Monitor and report. And that worked when programs were linear and time was abundant.

But in the AI Commercial Era, where Launchcode agents are continuously sensing and acting, governance cannot be episodic. It must be ever-present. Embedded. Dynamic.

In short, governance must evolve from a function into an operating model.

That means:

- **Rule enforcement is coded, not conversational.**

- **Oversight is continuous, not periodic.**

- **Transparency is real-time, not retrospective.**

And that's not just a technical adjustment. It's a cultural one. Commercial teams must learn to see governance not as friction, but as enablement. As the confidence layer that makes innovation sustainable and defensible.

Launch Is When Governance Matters Most

It's easy to assume that governance can be "tightened up" later. After launch. After scale. After AI agents are already in motion.

But the reality is: most governance failures don't come from malice. They come from momentum.

Launch pressure creates urgency. And urgency can tempt teams to skip safeguards in favor of speed.

But in an agentic system, where every node is activated simultaneously targeting, messaging, field, patient governance must be fully operational **on day one**.

Key Governance Questions at Launch:

- Have all content modules been pre-approved with usage tags?

- Are frequency and channel rules embedded in agent logic?

- Have off-label guardrails been tested across all agent workflows?

- Are escalation pathways mapped and tested for override scenarios?

- Are regional regulatory variations coded into localized agent behaviors?

Table 10.2: Launch Governance Checklist

Governance Area	Launch Readiness Requirement
Content Logic	Modular assets reviewed and tagged by indication and use
Targeting Rules	AI logic aligned to segmentation and risk tolerances
Frequency Limits	Embedded by channel, agent, and geography
Escalation Pathways	Trigger scenarios mapped, routes assigned
Consent Infrastructure	Patient and HCP permissions logged and mapped
Role Permissions	Dashboards and override tools segmented by function

When governance is ready at launch, agents can operate with full confidence, and brands can move fast without breaking trust.

Regional Governance in a Global System

Pharma is global, but compliance is local. A campaign that's fully compliant in the U.S. might violate GDPR in Europe or run afoul of China's data residency rules.

That's why Launchcode's governance layer is **regionally aware**.

- Agents adjust their behaviors based on local laws.

- Message sequences are scoped geographically.

- Patient data handling respects national thresholds.

- Role-based permissions ensure that only approved users see or act on data.

It's not just about language or localization.

It's about **regulatory DNA**. Governance must be adaptable coded not only for what agents can do, but **where and how they should do it**.

Governance Extends to Third Parties

Today's commercial systems don't operate in silos. They span ecosystems, hubs, pharmacies, CRMs, media platforms, call centers, and data brokers. And every handoff introduces risk.

So Launchcode treats governance **not as internal hygiene**, but as an ecosystem-wide mandate.

- APIs are permissioned and monitored.

- Partner actions are logged in the same audit trails as agent activity.

- Third-party vendors are required to follow approved logic paths and content rules.

- Data sharing agreements include tagging, usage restrictions, and retention policies.

When compliance extends beyond your walls, trust becomes **an architecture**, not a policy.

Audits in Seconds, Not Weeks

Ask any commercial leader about audit readiness, and you'll see a grimace. It's a slog gathering emails, rebuilding timelines, and explaining intent. It's slow. It's reactive. It's stressful.

But with Launchcode:

- Every decision is logged.

- Every logic path is saved.

- Every override is traceable.

- Every message is tagged and time-stamped.

Need to explain why a specific HCP received

the specific message on a specific date? One click reveals:

- The agent that made the decision.

- The signals used.

- The logic path taken.

- The content variant was delivered.

- The compliance tags are applied.

Audit becomes a capability, not a crisis.

Ethical Oversight: Beyond What's Legal

Compliance ensures legality. But ethics ensures **trustworthiness**.

And as AI takes on more responsibility, the ethical bar rises.

Questions we must ask:

- Are our models favoring high-income geographies?

- Are we respecting digital fatigue and consent boundaries?

- Are we surfacing equity gaps or hiding them through segmentation?

- Are patients and providers aware when AI is involved in their experience?

Launchcode's governance system includes:

- Bias detection dashboards.

- Fairness audits by demographic and geography.

- Patient-level opt-outs for AI-supported content.

- Transparency guidelines for AI disclosures.

Because in the end, AI isn't just about automation. It's about accountability.

Governance as a Strategic Differentiator

When embedded correctly, governance doesn't slow you down. It's what allows you to move faster, safer, and smarter.

- Faster approvals? Pre-tagged modules, not re-reviews.

- Bolder experimentation? Guardrails are in place.

- Partner confidence? Shared audit trails.

- Field alignment? Real-time monitoring with override rights.

Table 10.3: Strategic Benefits of Embedded Governance

Advantage	Enabled By
Fast launch cycles	Pre-configured assets and logic
Continuous optimization	Safe experimentation within compliance bounds
Audit simplicity	One-click traceability of every action
Ecosystem trust	Partner behavior is governed and visible
Global compliance	Region-specific logic blocks embedded in agents

This isn't about controlling the system. It's about empowering it, with trust baked in.

Final Thought

You don't scale intelligent systems with brute force.

You scale them with trust.

And trust doesn't come from promises. It comes from **governance that's designed, deployed, and demonstrated every single day**.

Launchcode doesn't just optimize action. It governs intention.

And in the future of pharmaceutical commercialization, that might be the most powerful agent of all.

Chapter 11: Launchcode in Action

From Pilot to Platform: The Proof Behind the Promise

The Moment of Proof

Frameworks are useful. Architecture diagrams are powerful. Agent definitions and decision logic bring clarity. But when it comes to adoption real adoption nothing speaks louder than proof. Not hypothetical examples. Not conceptual benefits. Actual stories. Real-world use cases. And measurable outcomes that leaders can see, teams can feel, and organizations can scale.

This chapter is that proof.

We're not talking about dashboards or incremental campaign tweaks. These case studies show intelligent orchestration in motion, how Launchcode works not just as a collection of tools, but as a commercial operating system. Across brands, across teams, across use cases.

This isn't a pitch deck. It's a playbook built from the field, validated by performance, and ready to scale.

Case Study 1: First-to-Market in Rare Neurology

The Setup

A mid-sized biotech company was preparing to launch a first-in-class gene therapy targeting a rare pediatric neuromuscular disease. Stakes were high:

- Population: Fewer than 10,000 eligible patients in the U.S.

- Diagnosis lag: 12 to 18 months, often due to symptom ambiguity.

- Reimbursement friction: The six-figure price tag triggered payer scrutiny.

- Channel complexity: Cold-chain logistics, nurse training, and genetic counseling.

- Knowledge gap: Many pediatric neurologists were unaware of diagnostic pathways.

Failure here wasn't just commercial. It meant delaying care for children with progressive, irreversible decline.

The Orchestration

Launchcode went live 60 days before approval. Every agent was activated in parallel, each playing a role in a launch strategy that felt more like choreography than execution.

Agent	Key Contribution
Targeting Agent	Flagged pediatric neurology centers with low historical engagement but high potential based on referral behavior and EMR data.
Messaging Agent	Sequenced a series of educational modules aligned to HCP awareness levels—disease-state first, mechanism second, logistics third.
Access Agent	Modeled prior auth friction by plan type and geography, enabling pre-launch coverage messaging.
Field Agent	Prioritized KOLs and low-awareness HCPs for early in-person engagement with objection handling prep.
Patient Agent	Triggered onboarding coordination for families post-script, escalating based on benefit verification delay or education fatigue.
Performance Agent	Monitored which signals drove adoption, which HCPs moved from awareness to action, and where conversion stalled.

The Outcome

- 92% of the forecast was achieved within the first 90 days.

- 36% decrease in average time-to-therapy compared to prior benchmarks.

- 7% re-education rate demonstrating the precision of message sequencing.

- 80% refill adherence despite complex administration.

This wasn't just a good launch. It was a system-driven launch one that outpaced historical benchmarks not by working harder, but by working smarter.

Case Study 2: Mid-Cycle Access Shock

The Setup

A cardiovascular brand, five years post-launch, began seeing a sharp TRx decline in key geographies. Field teams assumed competitive pressure. Marketing began preparing counter-detailing campaigns.

But Launchcode detected a different signal.

The Reveal

- **Access Agent** caught a formulary change from a Tier 2 to Tier 3 position at a dominant payer in four affected states.

- **Patient Agent** flagged a spike in onboarding drop-offs within 48 hours.

- **Messaging Agent** automatically swapped in co-pay and access materials approved and tagged for such scenarios.

- **Field Agent** reprioritized call plans based on ZIP code access disruption.

- **Performance Agent** tracked recovery, flagging underperforming segments for additional escalation.

Table 11.1: Traditional Field Model vs Field Agent Model

Aspect	Traditional Field Model	Field Agent Model
Call planning	Static, quarterly decile-based	Dynamic, updated daily based on a live signal
Message selection	Manual or CRM-driven	Sequenced by Messaging Agent, based on HCP behavior
Access insight	Manual hub review or rep knowledge	Triggered by Access Agent alerts
Digital coordination	Disconnected	Orchestrated across channels
Rep feedback	Post-cycle, subjective	Captured continuously, used to refine logic

The Outcome

- TRx decline halted within 10 business days.

- Rebound to 97% of prior levels within a month.

- 32% increase in rep confidence discussing access.

- 24-hour turnaround for co-pay guidance at point of drop-off.

With traditional tools, this would've taken 6–8 weeks to identify and another cycle to fix. Launchcode resolved it in less than one workweek without requiring a war room.

Case Study 3: Digital Fatigue in Oncology

The Setup

A top-five pharma company was mid-launch in oncology. They had invested heavily in digital channels, with impressive open rates and time-on-page initially.

Until they didn't.

By Q2, HCP engagement was down despite increasing volume. The team was preparing to double down.

Launchcode recommended the opposite.

The Diagnosis

- **Messaging Agent** flagged sequencing fatigue in top decile prescribers.

- **Field Agent** reported HCP pushback on message duplication.

- **Performance Agent** correlated declining engagement with TRx dips and surfaced a need for content refresh.

The Adjustment

- Messaging cadence cut by 25% in saturated territories.

- Content updated with ASCO-presented data modules.

- Field and digital outreach synchronized.

- Patient Agent created caregiver-facing assets to reduce HCP load.

Table 11.2: Messaging Coordination – impact on reps

Feature	Impact on Reps
Message sequencing	Builds narrative continuity across personal + digital
Channel suppression logic	Prevents HCP burnout and improves engagement quality
Performance feedback loop	Guides reps toward higher-performing messaging approaches
Cross-agent insights	Equips reps with reasons for disengagement or success

The Outcome

- 22% rise in CTR.

- 31% increase in time-on-page.

- 9% growth in net-new prescribers MoM.

- 60% reduction in HCP complaints about digital overload.

- Field + digital channel alignment improved rep satisfaction by >40%.

This wasn't just campaign tuning. It was full-system orchestration tuned to signal.

Operationalizing Orchestration at Scale

In a world where most pharma organizations struggle to scale their best practices, Launchcode turns pilots into platforms. What begins as targeted interventions, field improvement, messaging refinement, or patient support optimization can evolve into a systemic transformation across the portfolio. In this section, we zoom out from individual case studies to understand how intelligent orchestration impacts cross-brand execution, rep experience, rare disease scalability, and even corporate culture.

Case Study 4: Portfolio-Wide Rollout at a Top 20 Pharma

The Situation

A global pharma company with 15+ active brands faced the common dilemma: each brand functioned in isolation. Different teams. Different tools. Different truths. Despite significant investment in CRM, MLR workflows, and campaign analytics, inefficiencies mounted:

- Disconnected data pipelines.

- Redundant content production.

- Inconsistent field coordination.

- Compliance bottlenecks for every brand.

The Solution

Leadership opted to deploy Launchcode across its portfolio. Starting with oncology and immunology, they created shared governance structures and agent templates. Over six months, the platform was extended to additional brands, harmonizing the commercial model.

Table 11.3: Brand Functions Harmonized by Launchcode Across Portfolio

The Outcome

- 28% reduction in content production costs.

Function	Previous State	Post-Launch code State
Targeting	Decile-based, brand-defined	Dynamic, coordinated across brands
Messaging	Content silos managed per brand	Modular library with shared logic and tagging
Field strategy	CRM-driven with minimal transparency	Signal-driven call plans with system attribution
Access coordination	Managed manually by brand teams	Centralized Access Agent with payer intelligence integration
Analytics	Retrospective and brand-specific	Real-time, cross-brand dashboards with agent attribution

- 42% increase in rep engagement with call planning tools.

- 33% improvement in forecast accuracy across five brands.

- Faster brand onboarding and shorter MLR cycles.

This wasn't just digital transformation. It was commercial replatforming.

Case Study 5: Increasing Rep Satisfaction with Intelligent Orchestration

The Situation

At a mid-sized biotech, field team turnover had hit a record high. Reps felt like cogs in a machine:

- No visibility into whether their efforts mattered.

- Constant changes in call plans.

- Mixed messages from digital and field touchpoints.

- Pressure to hit KPIs without clarity or tools.

The Intervention

Instead of refreshing training programs, the company piloted the Field Agent. The results were immediate and dramatic.

Rep Experience Improvements

- Daily prioritized call lists based on real-time signal.

- Rep-level dashboards tying actions to business outcomes.

- Messaging coordinated with digital touchpoints.

- Feedback loop: reps could influence future call logic.

The Results

- 47% drop in voluntary turnover.

- TRx rose 18% in test territories.

- Rep trust in strategy rose from 3.2 to 4.7 (5-point scale).

- Managers shifted from activity review to strategic coaching.

Launchcode didn't just improve efficiency it gave reps purpose.

Case Study 6: Rare Disease Pilot with Limited Data

The Situation

A biotech entering the rare metabolic disease space faced a familiar constraint:

- Few prescribers.

- Minimal brand awareness.

- Almost no historical data.

The Fear

Would Launchcode even work without signal volume?

The Reality

The system adapted. Using surrogate signals like conference participation, diagnostic code trends, and EMR metadata the Targeting Agent identified early influencers. The Messaging Agent tested content in controlled waves. The Patient Agent filled gaps in field presence with digital and nurse-led onboarding support.

Table 11.4: How Launchcode Performs in Low-Data Environments

Challenge	Launch code Adaptation
Limited historical data	Surrogate targeting based on proxy behaviors
Small HCP base	Precision sequencing to minimize fatigue
Sparse field coverage	Virtual-first Field Agent deployment
Complex onboarding	Escalation paths via the Patient Agent

The Results

- 86% of identified HCPs engaged within 30 days.

- First-fill exceeded forecast by 19%.

- 31% drop in patient support escalations.

- Leadership greenlit Launchcode expansion.

Even in a data desert, intelligent orchestration found traction.

Patterns That Predict Performance

Across use cases, certain orchestration strategies repeatedly emerged as high performers. These "agentic patterns" became reusable playbooks instantly applicable across launches, therapeutic areas, and geographies.

Table 11.5: Common Agentic Patterns Across High-Performing Brands

Orchestration Pattern	Performance Outcome
Field + Messaging alignment	Higher HCP engagement, lower channel conflict
Access + Patient coordination	Faster time-to-therapy, reduced drop-off
Simulation pre-launch	Smoother execution, faster trajectory adjustments
Modular content tagging	Lower MLR friction, easier personalization at scale
Real-time override logic	Improved compliance trust, less friction at agent edges

Launchcode doesn't just automate. It teaches, repeats, and scales what works.

Final Word

What these cases show is not just technical success but a cultural shift.

- Brand teams stopped guessing.

- Field teams stopped flying blind.

- Commercial leadership stopped reviewing and started steering.

The system didn't replace strategy. It enhanced it with orchestration that was explainable, auditable, and adaptable.

Chapter 11 is proof that Launchcode isn't a tool. It's an operating model built for a world where speed, signal, and trust all matter more than ever.

Chapter 12: The Commercial Operating Model of the Future

From Static Structures to Dynamic Systems

The Commercial Model Is Cracking

For decades, the pharmaceutical industry ran on a familiar rhythm products were launched through annual brand plans, organized in functional silos, and executed via sprawling vendor ecosystems. The model thrived in an environment where everything was predictable: timelines, formularies, and engagement paths.

That world is gone.

Today's commercial environment looks nothing like the one those models were designed to support. It's faster. More fragmented. More complex. And it's exposing the limits of the traditional operating model at every turn.

- **Launch cycles have accelerated**, with more products entering the market across more indications and more nuanced segments.

- **Access friction has intensified**, as payers get more restrictive and policy changes outpace brand response.

- **HCP access has plummeted**, particularly in high-value academic centers, urban hubs, and integrated delivery networks.

- **Patients are digitally connected**, but their journeys are more fragmented than ever.

- **Marketing execution has become chaotic**, replacing centralized campaigns with an endless stream of micro-messages across platforms and partners.

- **Data is everywhere**, but most teams are still reliant on dashboards and slide decks, not real-time decision engines.

This isn't just a digital problem. It's a structural one.

Pharma's commercial systems were built for a different era. And no amount of patchwork optimization can keep up. It's not about tweaking the old model anymore.

It's about building a new one.

From Playbooks to Platforms

Launchcode doesn't just give you a new targeting algorithm or a smarter message engine. It offers something more foundational: a new operating model.

A model that's dynamic, not static.

Continuous, not episodic.

Coordinated, not siloed.

Systemic, not slide-based.

Let's break it down.

The Limits of Today's Commercial Model

Most commercial organizations still look something like this:

1. **Annual brand planning:** Linear Gantt charts, static segmentations, and rigid budget cycles.

2. **Functional silos:** Marketing, sales, access, and support teams working in parallel but rarely in sync.

3. **Vendor fragmentation:** Each brand manages its own ecosystem of agencies, data feeds, and tools.

4. **Lagging optimization:** Insights gathered after the fact, once quarterly reviews are complete.

5. **Governance bottlenecks:** MLR teams focused on reviewing final assets, not shaping strategy.

6. **Limited experimentation:** Testing is confined to A/B email subject lines or message variants in narrow pilots.

These systems were designed for control. But in today's market, **speed, intelligence, and orchestration** are what drive results.

Table 12.1: Traditional vs. Agentic Commercial Operating Model

Dimension	Traditional Model	Launch code Model
Planning cadence	Annual or semi-annual	Continuous, agent-refined
Decision-making	Human-led, slide-driven	Signal-driven, agent-augmented
Function coordination	Manual meetings	Agent-to-agent orchestration
Content deployment	Pre-scripted campaigns	Modular, rule-based delivery
Rep guidance	Static call plans	Dynamic, priority-based targeting
Governance	End-stage review	Embedded compliance logic

Rewriting the Org Chart

When intelligent agents take on core commercial functions, human roles evolve.

This isn't about reducing headcount. It's about redirecting talent away from manual execution and toward intelligent oversight. Launchcode transforms every seat on the commercial team into a more strategic, high-leverage role.

1. Marketers become System Designers

Instead of deploying campaigns, brand teams configure orchestration logic:

- What signals should the Targeting Agent act on?

- Which message variants are appropriate for which segments?

- When should Messaging or Access Agents escalate?

They move from "writing the plan" to "programming the system."

2. Sales Managers become Signal Coaches

Instead of auditing call volume or enforcing CRM discipline, sales leaders:

- Coach reps on interpreting and responding to the signal.

- Tune Field Agent logic based on what's working in-market.

- Shift from territory management to orchestration enablement.

3. MLR Teams become Compliance Architects

Rather than reviewing one asset at a time, MLR leaders:

- Define usage rules and risk tiers across message modules.

- Monitor exception alerts and approve escalations.

- Embed safeguards directly into agentic logic.

They move from bottlenecks to enablers speeding safe scale.

4. Data Teams become Performance Engineers

Analysts no longer just build dashboards. They:

- Maintain attribution models and signal calibration.

- Monitor drift in agent performance.

- Simulate launch scenarios and targeting shifts.

They become integral to the learning loop, not just its interpreter.

Table 12.2: Role Evolution in the AI Commercial Model

From Intervention to Orchestration

Traditional Role	New Role	Key Contribution
Brand Manager	Agent Strategy Lead	Configures orchestration logic, prioritization rules
Sales Manager	Signal Coach	Aligns reps to agent logic, enables system-driven performance
MLR Reviewer	Compliance Logic Architect	Builds rule sets, reviews system escalations
Analyst	Agent Performance Engineer	Calibrates models, interprets drift, and drives experimentation
Field Rep	Insight Amplifier	Executes with system guidance, closes context gaps

The most profound shift in this model isn't organizational. It's cultural.

Historically, confidence in pharma commercial teams has come from **control**:

- "Let me approve every asset before it goes out."
- "I need to sign off on the segmentation."
- "We'll launch once the whole plan is ready."

But in an agentic system, confidence comes from **orchestration**:

- Agents don't guess that they follow governed logic.
- Actions don't depend on meetings; they're triggered by a signal.
- Strategy isn't deployed in waves; it evolves in real time.

This shift from microcontrol to intelligent trust is the real unlock.

Because the new model doesn't just change what we do. It changes **how we think**.

Building the New Cross-Functional Core

Success in an agent-powered model doesn't come from adding more tools. It comes from realigning the team around a shared system and shared accountability.

In high-performing Launchcode implementations, a new kind of core team emerges:

- **Brand leads** configure the strategic parameters.
- **Ops teams** own the integration and rollout.

- **Analytics teams** run tuning, validation, and drift detection.

- **Field leadership** ensures rep alignment and adoption.

- **Medical and compliance** oversee risk, logic, and escalation.

- **Patient and access teams** co-orchestrate journeys.

These aren't passive stakeholders.

They're co-pilots of a living system.

What This Looks Like in Practice

Instead of reviewing quarterly metrics, the team tunes agent logic weekly. Instead of asking "why did this happen?" they ask "what can we adjust now?"

Instead of chasing KPIs, they orchestrate outcomes.

This is what it means to move from execution to orchestration. From campaigns to systems. From PowerPoints to platforms.

From Theory to Execution

The Hard Part Is the Transition

Understanding the vision is the easy part. A fully orchestrated, intelligent commercial model powered by Launchcode sounds great on paper. But making the leap to operationalizing it inside a real-world pharmaceutical organization is where the real work begins.

Why? Because pharma wasn't designed for adaptability.

The commercial function has been optimized for predictability: annual plans, fixed budgets, quarterly reviews, and narrowly scoped brand roles. Legacy systems, entrenched mindsets, and compliance bottlenecks weren't just obstacles; and they were design features.

To bring Launchcode to life, organizations must move beyond transformation theater. They need to reprogram the logic of commercialization itself.

But here's the good news: You don't have to blow up your operating model overnight.

You can start small. You can start smart.

You just have to start.

Start Small, But Start Smart

The most successful agentic transformations begin with a focused use case: one brand, one region, one problem that traditional models have failed to solve.

High-impact starting points include:

Use Case	Why It Works
Launch preparation	Clean slate, limited legacy workflows
Access performance	Tangible ROI from reducing friction
Messaging personalization	Rapid deployment and visible HCP impact
Rare disease	Small data sets, high stakes, quick feedback

The key to early momentum isn't breadth. It's clarity.

Define the problem precisely:

- Is it a drop in time-to-therapy?

- A missed TRx forecast?

- A rep engagement issue?

Then configure the agents to respond. Let them learn. Let them show impact.

Nothing builds organizational confidence like a system that adapts on its own.

Assemble the Right Implementation Core

Even the best technology fails without a strong cross-functional launch team. We've seen this time and time again: pilot programs flounder not because the system didn't work, but because no one owned the orchestration.

Think of this team as your internal Launchcode command center. It should include:

- **Commercial Lead** – Owns outcomes, sets direction.

- **Operations Owner** – Manages rollout cadence and tooling.

- **IT/Data Liaison** – Ensures data access and system connectivity.

- **Compliance Partner** – Validates rule logic and audit readiness.

- **Brand Strategist** – Guides message configuration and targeting logic.

- **Field Force Leader** – Bridges rep workflows and adoption.

This isn't just a project team.

It's the group that reprograms how your commercial system thinks.

Table 12.3: Key Roles in an Agentic Transition

Role	Responsibility
Commercial lead	Aligns agent behavior to business KPIs
Ops coordinator	Manages sprints, adoption checkpoints
IT/Data partner	Enables integrations and data cleanliness
Compliance lead	Embeds rules, governs experimentation.
Brand strategist	Curates content, segmentation inputs
Field lead	Champions rep alignment and training

This team doesn't "implement software."

They redesign your commercialization logic.

Shift Workflows, Not Just Technology

A successful agentic rollout doesn't just turn on Launchcode. It changes how people work with it.

5 Foundational Workflow Shifts:

From	To
Campaign creation	Logic configuration and rule design
Call plans	Daily orchestration based on HCP signal
Post-hoc reviews	Real-time dashboards and alerts
Review queues	Exception management with audit trails
Segmentation slides	Live behavior-driven targeting

These changes are more than process tweaks.

They redefine how value is created and who gets to create it.

Train for Roles That Didn't Exist Before

Once you shift workflows, new skillsets start to emerge. Teams need to be equipped not just with software training, but with a whole new fluency in co-piloting intelligent systems.

Core Capabilities to Build:

- **Agent Logic Configuration** – Curating triggers, thresholds, and escalation logic.

- **Performance Interpretation** – Understanding what agent metrics actually mean.

- **Signal Response Prioritization** – Knowing when to act, escalate, or suppress.

- **Governance Scenario Modeling** – Defining rules for edge cases and overrides.

- **Human–AI Collaboration** – Learning when to trust the system and when to override it.

This isn't just change management.

It's capability building for a new generation of commercial leadership.

Training Focus Areas

Focus Area	What to Teach
Mindset	How orchestration works and why it matters
Tool Fluency	How to interpret agent output, dashboards, and drift
Scenario Navigation	Common decisions and override moments
Cross-Functional Empathy	How agents depend on upstream/downstream inputs

You're not teaching the team how to operate software. You're teaching them how to **think in systems**.

Governance Must Shift from Review to Resilience

One of the most critical transformations in the Launchcode model is governance. In legacy systems, governance is a gate. It reviews what's already been created.

In an agentic system, governance is a **set of embedded rules** that shape system behavior from the start.

Principles of Modern Commercial Governance:

1. **Rules over Review**

   - Agents follow hardcoded logic no manual approvals required.

2. **Traceability and Explainability**

   - Every action is logged, auditable, and attributable.

3. **Threshold Alerts**

   - Humans review only what exceeds risk tolerance.

4. **Model Drift Monitoring**

   - The system flags when behavior diverges from logic.

5. **Consent Verification**

   - Patients and HCPs remain in control of outreach permissions.

6. **Human-in-the-Loop Overrides**

- Sensitive actions are escalated before execution. Governance doesn't go away.

  It gets **smarter, safer, and more scalable.**

Table 12.4: Governance Maturity Model

Stage	Key Characteristics
Manual review	MLR queues, long review cycles
Rule-based moderation	Content usage rules, frequency caps
Embedded compliance	Predefined thresholds in agent logic
Predictive governance	Drift detection, override protocol embedded

Executive Sponsorship: The Hidden Accelerator

No agentic transformation scales without strong executive backing. This isn't an ops project. It's a leadership imperative.

Executives must:

- **Champion the Vision** – Articulate the shift from static to system.

- **Fund the Transition** – Invest in infrastructure, roles, and change management.

- **Shield the Early Teams** – Protect pilots from unrealistic expectations.

- **Model the Behavior** – Use agent dashboards, adopt system language.

- **Make it Strategic** – Tie orchestration to P&L, launch excellence, and competitive advantage.

When executives treat Launchcode as a core operating system, not an innovation theater, it creates permission, clarity, and momentum.

Scale with Confidence

Once you prove early success, scaling doesn't mean rebuilding. It means replicating what works.

Keys to sustainable scale:

- Codify agent logic templates (e.g., targeting playbooks, messaging sequences).

- Standardize governance and escalation rules.

- Expand modular content libraries.

- Enable brand teams to configure without engineering.

- Harmonize dashboards for cross-brand visibility.

- Use the Performance Agent to identify high-performing patterns across launches.

Each brand makes the system smarter.

Each rollout makes the next one faster.

Final Word: From Static to Systemic

Pharmaceutical commercialization was designed for a world that no longer exists.

It was built to control when what we need now is the ability to coordinate. It was built to report when what we need now is the ability to respond. It was built to plan when what we need now is the ability to learn.

Launchcode offers more than technology.

It offers a reimagined commercial system:

- Where marketers program behavior instead of deploying campaigns.

- Where reps operate with clarity, not guesswork.

- Where compliance is embedded, not imposed.

- Where data fuels decisions, not just dashboards.

- Where brands launch faster, engage smarter, and improve continuously.

You don't need to change everything overnight.

But once you see how orchestration works, you'll never want to go back.

This is not just evolution. This is a new operating era.

Chapter 13: Reimagining the Role of Commercial Leadership

From Command and Control to System-Oriented Stewardship

A New Kind of Leadership Moment

Pharmaceutical commercial leaders have historically succeeded by mastering a complex, high-stakes, and often slow-moving operating model. They've built careers around navigating matrixed teams, balancing brand priorities, managing field forces, and negotiating with access and medical stakeholders.

But today's environment isn't just complex it's volatile, interconnected, and increasingly intelligent.

What worked in a world of annual brand plans and quarterly reviews no longer works when:

- Systems adapt faster than review cycles.

- Messages change daily based on the signal.

- Reps are guided by real-time prioritization.

- Campaigns are tuned by learning loops, not top-down strategy.

- Compliance is embedded in logic, not layered on top.

And that means commercial leadership itself must evolve not incrementally, but fundamentally.

The Legacy Commercial Leadership Playbook

In the traditional model, commercial leaders were architects and overseers. They:

- Owned P&L and launch timelines.

- Defined brand plans and tactical calendars.

- Sponsored agency relationships and data vendors.

- Managed field deployment, incentive design, and resourcing.

- Made decisions in meetings, reviews, and escalation pathways.

- Served as final approvers for content, strategy, and segmentation.

Leadership in this model was about managing outputs: plans, messages, materials, and meetings. It was slide-driven, top-down, and milestone-based.

But the agent-powered model doesn't run on quarterly cycles or strategy decks.

It runs on signals and orchestration.

Table 13.1: Traditional vs. Agent-Era Commercial Leadership

Leadership Attribute	Traditional Model	Launch code Model
Decision cadence	Monthly or quarterly	Real-time, continuous
Oversight method	Review of outputs and reports	Embedded dashboards, orchestration diagnostics
Influence style	Directive and top-down	Systemic, tuning agent logic and configuration rules
Performance focus	Execution of the plan	Outcome optimization and agent adaptability
Collaboration mechanism	Steering committees and war rooms	Continuous cross-agent alignment and signal calibration
Compliance role	Final approver	Rule architect and escalation designer

From Strategic Architect to System Orchestrator

The new model requires leaders to engage differently. They don't direct every action. Instead, they create the logic that the system executes:

- **Architect orchestration logic**: Define rules and thresholds that guide agents.

- **Curate signal priorities**: Choose which behaviors, geographies, or moments deserve emphasis.

- **Oversee alignment**: Ensure messaging, targeting, access, and field agents reinforce, not contradict each other.

- **Interpret system behavior**: Read dashboards to identify performance drift, friction, or fatigue.

- **Sponsor experimentation**: Approve controlled testing and tune performance rules based on results.

This is leadership not by mandate, but by tuning the same way a conductor adjusts tempo or tone based on how the orchestra plays.

It's an evolution in posture: from seeing themselves as decision-makers to becoming designers of decision systems.

Leadership Mindset Shifts

Adopting the Launchcode model requires more than new dashboards. It requires new instincts.

1. From Intuition to Attribution

Old model: "We know this works, it's what we used last launch."

New model: "The data tells us what's working, let's follow the signal."

This transition can be uncomfortable, especially for seasoned executives who built their careers on pattern recognition and gut calls. But attribution isn't a challenge to experience. It's a magnifier of what works.

2. From Alignment to Calibration

Old model: "Let's align the plan across functions."

New model: "Let's calibrate agent logic to execute the same intent."

Calibration doesn't just reduce friction. It creates harmony across functions, geographies, and segments so the system speaks with one voice.

3. From Approval to Enablement

Old model: "I'll approve the message and call plan."

New model: "I'll set the rules the system uses to deploy both."

Enablement doesn't mean letting go of control, it means reshaping control as intentional design.

4. From Retrospective to Real-Time

Old model: "Let's review performance at the end of the quarter."

New model: "Let's detect performance drift and course-correct now."

Speed isn't the enemy of safety; it's the ally of agility, especially when change is embedded in controlled systems.

Leading in a System of Agents

The presence of autonomous agents doesn't make leadership obsolete. It makes it more strategic.

Agents can:

- Prioritize actions.

- Sequence messages.

- Detect drift and fatigue.

- Adjust outreach across channels.

- Measure attribution at scale.

But they can't:

- Interpret nuance or strategic ambiguity.

- Balance reputational and ethical trade-offs.

- Shape culture, incentives, or trust.

- Navigate institutional constraints.

- Drive long-term investment tradeoffs.

Great leadership now means partnering with the system, not directing every move, but designing the architecture through which intelligent action happens.

It also requires emotional intelligence. Systems can analyze behavior, but they can't sense anxiety. They don't build trust or inspire mission. That's still the job of the human leader to build psychological safety amid transformation.

Table 13.2: Key Components of an Executive-Oriented Leadership Dashboard

Component	What It Shows
Agent Performance Panel	Effectiveness of each agent (e.g., TRx lift from targeting logic)
Signal Velocity Indicator	Speed at which the system detects and acts on behavioral change
Alignment Heat maps	Degree of coordination across agents by geography or segment
Override Logs	Where humans stepped in—what changed, and why
Intervention ROI Tracker	Yield from key campaign decisions triggered by agent signal

Coaching the System

Just as managers coach their teams, leaders coach the system.

Table 13.3: Commercial Leadership Levers in the Agentic Model

System Lever	Leadership Input
Agent priority weighting	Shift the balance between access, targeting, and field.
Sequencing logic	Approve new message or campaign pathways.
Risk tolerance thresholds	Configure compliance trigger points.
Override parameters	Decide when human review must pause or redirect logic.
Experimentation enablement	Authorize live testing and control models.

This is where leadership becomes a high-leverage discipline. It's not about attending every meeting. It's about making every signal smarter, every sequence more strategic, and every agent more aligned.

The Leadership Team, Reimagined

Leadership teams now function less like approval boards and more like orchestration command centers. They:

- Interpret orchestration dashboards.

- Identify cross-agent misalignment.

- Approve strategic rule changes.

- Discuss escalation scenarios.

- Track system drift and performance variance.

In the old world, alignment meant consensus. In the new world, it means system coherence.

And the fastest way to break coherence? Competing logic sets where brand, field, and access each run their own rules.

In this model, leadership isn't about holding court. It's about sharing control with machines, with teams, and with each other.

Table 13.4: Traditional vs. Agent-Era Leadership Team Rhythm

Traditional Rhythm	Agent-Era Rhythm
Quarterly brand reviews	Real-time signal dashboards
Monthly field performance meetings	Daily rep-agent alignment tracking
Annual segmentation updates	Weekly prioritization tuning
MLR-triggered stand-downs	Live compliance escalation and rollback options

Leadership in the AI Commercial Era is no longer about holding the reins of every decision. It's about designing the reins embedding strategy into the system, shaping the logic, and empowering teams to operate at market speed.

The best commercial leaders won't just manage better.

They'll lead differently. And in doing so, they won't just keep up with the pace of change they'll set it.

New Tools, New Metrics, New Mandates

Leading with a New Dashboard

The transition to Launchcode doesn't just change how decisions get made it transforms how leaders visualize, interpret, and act on performance. In the legacy model, insight was derived from static metrics: TRx trends, call activity, email opens, and PowerPoint dashboards that were weeks out of date. In the agent-powered model, leaders operate from a living dashboard one that reflects the current and cumulative orchestration of the system.

This is not just an increase in data. It's a new way of seeing the business.

Table 13.5: Components of the Agentic Executive Dashboard

Component	What It Shows
Agent Performance Panel	Effectiveness of each agent (Targeting, Messaging, Field, Access, Patient)
Alignment Heat maps	Degree of synchronization across agents by segment or region
Signal Velocity Indicator	Speed at which market signals are detected and acted upon
Governance Alert Log	Escalations, overrides, or pauses triggered by agent activity
ROI by Intervention Path	Financial impact of agent-triggered interventions
Human Override Record	Points where human input altered agentic decision pathways

These tools give leaders real-time visibility into what's working, what's not, and where to intervene not through oversight, but through intelligent system tuning.

Agentic KPIs: A New Vocabulary of Performance

Classic commercial KPIs reach, frequency, and scripts are still part of the picture, but they don't tell the full story. In a fully orchestrated system, leaders must shift their attention from outputs to orchestration quality.

Table 13.6: Traditional vs. Agentic KPIs

Traditional Metric	Why It Falls Short	Agentic KPI	Why It Matters
Call volume	Measures activity, not impact	Rep-Agent Alignment Score	Measures how effectively reps follow agent guidance
Email open rates	Doesn't reflect behavioral change	Message Lift Index	Measures message contribution to script growth
TRx by geography	Hard to attribute to any specific driver	Agent Influence by Region	Connects agent actions to market outcomes
Budget burn	Tracks spend, not performance	Intervention ROI	Shows return per system-triggered action
Segmentation accuracy	Based on static assumptions	Signal Responsiveness Index	Measures how well the system adjusts to live HCP or patient behavior

These KPIs are not just more granular they enable precision decisions. They give leaders confidence to adapt strategy based on agent-informed reality, not retrospective speculation.

From Mandates to Tuning

Legacy leadership models were built around mandates: "Hit these targets. Make these calls. Launch this campaign." In Launchcode, those directives are replaced by tunable rulesets, weighting mechanisms, and orchestration logic. It's less about controlling activity and more about influencing how the system sees and responds to reality.

Strategic leadership becomes a matter of tuning agent behavior across key leverage points:

Table 13.7: Strategic Levers for Agentic Commercial Leadership

System Lever	Leadership Input
Agent priority weighting	Adjust balance across targeting, access, field, and patient actions
Sequencing logic	Approve new sequencing tests or refine based on signal decay
Performance thresholds	Set system alerts when key metrics exceed or drop below tolerance
Channel override triggers	Define when the system should switch from digital to field—or vice versa
Escalation rules	Configure when human intervention is required based on risk level

This tuning model is not a loss of control it's an evolution of control. One that allows leaders to shape commercial momentum in real time, through logic, not latency.

Coaching a System, Not Just a Team

In the old model, coaching meant giving reps talking points, reviewing KPIs, and inspecting CRM behavior. In the agentic model, coaching includes optimizing the human-system interface. Reps, brand leads, and access managers all interact with agent logic and that interface is where high performance emerges.

Table 13.8: Coaching for System-Enhanced Commercial Roles

Role	Old Coaching Focus	New Coaching Focus
Field Rep	Call volume, message recall	Use of agent insights, quality of in-call interventions
Brand Manager	Campaign execution	Calibration of logic rules, signal thresholds, content tags
Access Lead	Payer navigation	Speed and accuracy of response to Access Agent alerts
Analyst	Dashboard delivery	Attribution accuracy, system learning loops
Sales Manager	Activity tracking	Signal tuning, agent alignment, orchestration fidelity

Coaching in the new model focuses on synergy: between human judgment and system recommendation, between rep action and agent logic.

Avoiding Leadership Pitfalls in the Agentic Era

As organizations make the leap to agent-powered orchestration, leadership missteps can stall momentum. Here are five common mistakes and how to avoid them.

Table 13.9: Common Pitfalls for Agent-Era Commercial Leaders

Pitfall	Impact	Corrective Shift
Treating agents as automation tools	Misses the orchestration opportunity	Reframe as a coordination layer, not a campaign scheduler
Clinging to manual approvals	Bottlenecks, speed, and learning loops	Focus on tuning input rules instead of inspecting outputs
Overriding agent decisions too early	Interrupts adaptive learning	Use Performance Agent to validate intervention thresholds
Sticking with legacy KPIs	Obscures orchestration gaps and lifts	Adopt agent-specific KPIs that reflect system behavior
Ignoring the cultural shift	Undermines adoption across teams	Model agent usage, speak the language of orchestration

Final Word

The next generation of commercial leadership will not be defined by how much they direct but by how well they tune. Leaders who embrace this shift will do more than drive brand performance. They will become system stewards calibrating intelligent infrastructure to reflect strategy, support the field, and amplify every interaction across the commercialization lifecycle.

This isn't a handoff to AI. It's a handshake.

A new compact between human intelligence and machine orchestration, working in lockstep to deliver outcomes that are not only better, but faster, safer, and more trusted.

Chapter 14: The Future of Commercial Talent in the AI Era

Rewriting the Commercial Job Description

When Talent Strategy Becomes System Strategy

AI isn't just transforming pharmaceutical commercialization through automation, and it's redefining the very nature of commercial work.

Historically, commercial teams thrived in clearly delineated roles. Marketers launched campaigns. Reps built relationships with providers. Access teams negotiated coverage. Analysts built dashboards. MSLs are educated clinicians. Each role lived in its own lane, measured by legacy KPIs and guided by static playbooks.

But in an agent-powered world, those lanes blur and new ones emerge entirely.

Today, agents handle:

- Repetitive targeting decisions.
- Sequencing of messaging across channels.
- Rep guidance and call plan optimization.
- Real-time compliance enforcement.
- Content deployment and feedback loops.
- Payer signal detection and patient support triggers.

So what's left for humans?

Plenty but it's different. The highest-value commercial professionals no longer drive execution directly. They orchestrate, interpret, configure, and refine the systems that do.

From Hands-On to System-In

In the old world, deep brand knowledge and functional expertise were the coin of the realm. But the agentic model values:

- Cross-functional fluency.

- Comfort working with dynamic systems.

- Curiosity about technology.

- Willingness to test, learn, and adapt.

- Skill in shaping the system's behavior, not just responding to it.

This isn't just a change in the toolkit. It's a shift in mindset from doing the work to guiding the system that does the work.

This shift also challenges long-held assumptions about what talent looks like, how success is measured, and what a career path in pharma should be.

And it opens the door for a different kind of professional one less defined by years in industry and more by adaptability, systems thinking, and a new form of leadership: co-piloting intelligent infrastructure.

Legacy Roles Are Evolving Fast

Roles aren't disappearing. But their definitions are evolving dramatically. Let's take a closer look at what that actually means across the commercial organization.

Table 14.1: Traditional Commercial Roles vs. Agent-Era Roles

Traditional Role	Legacy Focus	New Focus in AI-Enabled Model
Brand Manager	Tactical campaign delivery	Agent configuration, logic tuning, and rule orchestration
Sales Representative	Call frequency and detail aid recall	Agent-guided signal response and insight amplification
Field Manager	Call plan enforcement	Rep-agent alignment, coaching and performance interpretation
Digital Marketer	Channel-specific execution	Cross-agent coordination and modular content management
Access Lead	Contract negotiation and payer pull-through	Real-time signal interpretation and agent rule calibration
Data Analyst	Dashboard creation and report delivery	Agent performance tuning, model drift detection, signal analysis
MLR Reviewer	Pre-approval of content assets	Governance rule creation, escalation protocol design
Trainer	SOP and objection handling	Agent collaboration fluency, signal-based decision coaching
Operations Lead	Workflow optimization	System integration management and orchestration enablement
Medical Affairs Liaison	Clinical education	Signal-sensitive content modulation and scientific integrity oversight

This table reveals more than a set of evolving responsibilities it highlights a fundamental inversion. Execution becomes the domain of agents. Interpretation and orchestration become the domain of people.

The Rise of Hybrid Talent

As agents automate large portions of traditional workflows, a new kind of commercial professional is emerging one who understands both strategy and systems.

These hybrid roles bridge functional expertise and technical fluency:

- **Orchestration Strategists** configure how agents work together across the field, digital, access, and patient support.

- **Agent Performance Managers** monitor outcomes and tune behavior in real time.

- **Modular Content Programmers** design atomized content pieces tagged for intelligent use.

- **Compliance Architects** embed MLR rules and risk tiers into the orchestration logic.

- **Commercial Simulation Leads** model system behavior under different scenarios using the Performance Agent.

In short, the fastest-growing jobs in pharma commercialization didn't exist five years ago.

These roles don't replace traditional expertise they amplify it. A rep with 15 years of cardiology experience becomes exponentially more valuable when they can also interpret signal drift, re-weight field priorities in coordination with the system, and coach their peers to do the same.

What Skills Matter Now?

Success in this new environment requires a very different mix of capabilities.

Core Competencies for the AI-Era Commercial Team:

Skill Area	Description
Systemic Thinking	Understanding how commercial functions interact through agentic orchestration
Signal Interpretation	Reading dashboards, feedback loops, and alerts—not just reports
Experimentation Fluency	Designing and interpreting live tests to optimize system behavior
Rule Configuration	Translating brand strategy into agent-executable logic
Cross-Agent Collaboration	Understanding handoffs between Messaging, Field, Access, and Patient Agents
Tech-Human Translation	Explaining agentic decisions to stakeholders in plain business terms
Ethical Judgment	Recognizing when to override the system or trigger human escalation

These are no longer "future" skills. They're table stakes for thriving in an intelligent commercial system.

And for leaders building teams, these are the criteria that matter more than past job titles or historical performance.

Rethinking What "Top Talent" Looks Like

Legacy hiring practices favored:

- Deep experience in a specific therapeutic area.

- Familiarity with pharma SOPs.

- Campaign execution and field success.

- Time-in-role as a proxy for trustworthiness.

In contrast, the agentic model elevates:

- Comfort working with autonomous systems.

- Curiosity about experimentation and feedback.

- Agility in interpreting performance signals.

- Empathy for system users patients, reps, HCPs.

It also broadens the aperture for who can succeed. Talent from SaaS, tech-enabled consulting, behavioral science, UX design, compliance automation, or product management is often better prepared for Launchcode than traditional pharma lifers.

And that means recruiting, onboarding, and career development strategies must be rethought from the ground up.

Cross-Training for the System Era

One promising shift we're already seeing is the emergence of cross-training cohorts: rotational programs or task forces where field reps, analysts, and marketers temporarily switch roles to gain a system perspective.

In one organization, reps shadow the agent configuration team to understand how call lists are generated, then return to the field better equipped to interpret priorities. In another, brand marketers are embedded with patient support teams to experience how downstream messaging and onboarding logic are applied.

The effect is twofold:

1. **Empathy deepens** people gain insight into how their function fits into a broader orchestration.

2. **Capability expands** employees begin to speak the same "system language," enabling smoother collaboration and faster tuning cycles.

As we move on, we'll explore how this new talent model is shaping everything from career paths to coaching models, performance measurement, and cultural transformation.

Because Launchcode isn't just software.

It's a new way of thinking about people, potential, and progress.

From Capabilities to Culture

We've explored the shift in skills and roles needed to thrive in a commercial organization powered by Launchcode. But capability transformation isn't enough. For AI-enabled commercialization to scale, talent culture must evolve, too.

This means moving beyond tools and job descriptions. It requires:

- New mental models.

- New expectations around collaboration.

- A shared language around agents and signals.

- Clear, achievable paths for growth even as old hierarchies fade.

At the heart of it all? A deep belief that humans and intelligent systems can and must learn together.

Coaching for Roles That Didn't Exist

Traditional pharma coaching focused on tactical excellence:

- Reps were coached on call execution and objection handling.

- Brand teams were coached on campaign planning and agency management.

- Analysts were coached on dashboard delivery and PowerPoint storytelling.

But the agent-powered system demands something different.

Coaching now means helping people learn to:

- Interpret the system signal.

- Trust automation while recognizing drift.

- Escalate ethically when edge cases emerge.

- Tweak rules and thresholds for performance.

- Collaborate across functions through shared orchestration frameworks.

This is conceptual coaching, not just functional. It's not about "what" to do, it's about how to think in a world that's always adapting.

Table 14.2: Old vs. New Coaching Models in Pharma Commercial Roles

Role	Traditional Coaching	Agent-Era Coaching
Sales Rep	Detail accuracy, objection handling	Agent-guided call interpretation, signal response timing
Brand Marketer	Campaign execution, content review	Agent rule definition, performance signal tuning
Field Manager	Call plan compliance, incentive structure	System-guided coaching via rep–agent alignment metrics
MLR Reviewer	Asset checklists, claim substantiation	Governance configuration, scenario modeling
Analyst	Report formatting, stakeholder management	Agent performance interpretation, logic loop refinement

The best managers aren't supervising people.

They're developing humans who collaborate with machines.

Rethinking Performance Management

How do you measure commercial success when so much of the system is autonomous?

It starts by shifting from activity-based metrics (calls made, emails sent) to impact-based, system-aware metrics for both individuals and teams.

Key Individual Performance Metrics in the Agentic Model:

Role	Performance Signal
Rep	Adherence to agent prioritization; post-call impact
Marketer	Lift from agent-guided message variants and sequencing
Access Manager	Reduction in time-to-therapy through Access Agent inputs
Analyst	Speed and quality of system tuning and logic iteration
MLR Partner	% of flagged scenarios resolved via embedded governance

Key Team Performance Metrics:

- Agent coordination effectiveness.

- Response time to signal drift.

- Speed of experimentation cycle.

- System override rate (lower is better, unless by design).

- Escalation resolution speed and clarity.

- Cross-functional orchestration score (tracked by Performance Agent).

In short, commercial success is measured not by how much you do but by how well you tune, interpret, and trust the system you've helped build.

Retention in a World of System-Oriented Talent

There's a counterintuitive truth about Launchcode:

As more decisions become automated, top talent becomes even more important.

Why?

Because:

- Systems are only as good as the rules humans configure.

- Escalations require human judgment.

- Governance needs moral and clinical oversight.

- Agent tuning requires deep empathy for both users and data.

- Innovation happens where people and technology meet, not in isolation.

So the companies that retain their best people aren't the ones offering the most perks or the highest salaries.

They're the ones that:

- Give employees clarity of role in an evolving system.

- Offer coaching and experimentation paths for emerging roles.

- Celebrate orchestration wins, not just commercial ones.

- Invest in growth, not just tasks.

Retention is no longer about compensation alone. It's about creating purpose and mastery in a new system of value creation.

Managing the Emotional Side of Change

The shift to an AI-enabled model brings with it a very real emotional toll especially for experienced commercial professionals.

Common concerns include:

- "Will my job still exist in five years?"

- "If I don't write the plan, what value do I add?"

- "How do I stay relevant in a system I don't fully understand?"

- "Am I supposed to trust these agents more than my team?"

- "Is this another transformation that will stall or fade?"

Addressing these questions openly and empathetically is a leadership imperative.

Tactics that work:

- Host open forums on system ethics, autonomy, and accountability.

- Share agent win/loss stories to demystify the system.

- Acknowledge discomfort as a sign of growth, not weakness.

- Offer non-technical tracks for system-savvy leadership.

- Create "agent interpretation" certifications to build confidence.

Culture transformation isn't about pushing change, and it's about earning trust. And that starts with honesty, transparency, and inclusion.

Talent and the Feedback Loop

Launchcode isn't just an operating system, and it's also a talent development engine.

Because every agentic interaction is tracked, interpreted, and attributable, the system creates **automatic learning loops** for commercial professionals.

Examples:

- Reps can review not just whether they "hit their numbers," but how well they acted on agent recommendations.

- Marketers can A/B test their own logic changes and see the immediate impact.

- Analysts can run agent performance diagnostics and propose logic re-weightings.

- Managers can flag rising stars based on system fluency, not just charisma or tenure.

The Performance Agent doesn't just improve commercial outcomes.

It accelerates professional growth if you build the right dashboards and coach to them.

Embedding a Learning Culture

To make this all stick, organizations must shift from training as an event to learning as an operating rhythm.

How to Embed Continuous Talent Learning:

Practice	Impact
Weekly "Signal Review" huddles	Keeps teams fluent in agent feedback and pattern recognition
Monthly "System Tuning Days"	Encourages hands-on experimentation with agent rules and logic
Agentic Onboarding Curriculum	Gets new hires fluent in system dynamics before functional tactics
"What We Learned From the Agents" forum	Promotes cross-team sharing of insights and adaptations
Quarterly System Alignment Retreats	Replaces static planning with dynamic configuration workshops

This creates a workforce that doesn't just accept AI, it thrives because of it.

Final Word

Talent is the lever that will determine which pharmaceutical companies thrive in the AI commercial era.

Not the talent that can execute faster.

Not the talent that has the most experience.

But the talent that can:

- Learn how intelligent systems work.

- Guide them with empathy and purpose.

- Interpret their outputs with nuance.

- Intervene when needed and stay out of the way when not.

- And most importantly, bring humanity to a system designed for speed.

In the end, Launchcode isn't just about technology. It's about building the kind of organization where people and AI make each other better.

And if you get your talent model right?

The rest will follow.

Chapter 15: Designing for Trust

The Architecture of Integrity in an AI-Driven Commercial System

Trust Is the New Operating Requirement

In every conversation about AI in pharma, the same question bubbles just beneath the surface:

"Can we trust it?"

Not "Can it work?"

Not "Will it scale?"

Not even "What will it replace?"

But:

Can we trust the system that's making or influencing thousands of commercial decisions a day?

It's the right question. Because in healthcare, trust is currency. Providers, patients, regulators, and payers don't reward innovation unless they believe it's **safe, fair, and accountable**.

That's why designing for trust isn't an afterthought. It's the foundational principle of intelligent commercialization.

Launchcode doesn't just run fast.

It runs transparently, ethically, and explainably by design.

From Governance as Oversight to Trust as Infrastructure

Historically, trust in pharma commercialization was governed through layers of human oversight:

- Brand plans reviewed by leadership.

- Campaigns reviewed by agencies.

- Content reviewed by MLR.

- Field activity monitored post-hoc.

- CRM notes are audited periodically.

But that approach assumes a world where decisions are:

- Few.

- Linear.

- Human-made.

- Easy to trace after the fact.

In the Launchcode model, decisions are:

- Frequent thousands of content combinations and targeting actions per day.

- Adaptive driven by shifting signal and logic thresholds.

- Agentic, partially or fully autonomous.

- Distributed across systems, functions, and regions.

So, how do you replace manual review with systemic trust?

You don't. You embed trust into every layer of the platform, every configuration choice, and every escalation rule.

The Five Pillars of Trust in the Launchcode Era

To design for trust in an AI-powered commercialization system, you need more than compliance. You need a **robust, multidimensional trust framework** that spans ethics, transparency, explainability, safety, and control.

Pillar 1: Transparency

Everyone knows what the system is doing and why.

- Every action is logged.
- Every logic pathway is visible.
- Every signal input can be traced.
- Teams don't guess. They **see.**

Transparency means reps know why an HCP showed up in their call list.

It means compliance can validate why a message was deployed in Region X.

It means brand leads can retrace every agent decision, from targeting to messaging, without filing a ticket.

Pillar 2: Explainability

You can't trust what you can't explain.

Every recommendation an agent makes comes with a **natural language rationale**:

- What signals triggered this action?
- What other options were considered?
- Why was this path chosen?

Explainability transforms AI from a black box into a **strategic collaborator**.

It ensures that intelligent systems aren't just correct they're accountable.

Pillar 3: Control

Humans always retain the ability to override, escalate, or pause.

- Thresholds are adjustable.

- Risk tiers are encoded.

- Emergency stop protocols are system-wide.

Agents don't run wild. They run **within a governed perimeter** defined by your teams.

Pillar 4: Fairness

Bias isn't just a technical flaw. It's a trust killer.

Launchcode includes embedded fairness monitors:

- Performance Agent evaluates outcomes by geography, specialty, and demographic indicators.

- Access Agent checks for disparities in resource allocation.

- Messaging Agent flags imbalance in engagement lift by HCP tier.

Fairness isn't assumed. It's **measured and corrected.**

Pillar 5: Ethical Alignment

Launchcode doesn't just execute campaigns. It reflects your **values.**

Agents are configured to:

- Respect patient and HCP opt-outs.

- Avoid over-communication and coercive messaging.

- Prioritize patient dignity and clinical appropriateness.

Ethics isn't something you bolt on. It's something you **build into the logic itself**.

Table 15.1: Compliance vs. Trust in AI-Powered Commercial Models

Dimension	Traditional Compliance	Launch code Trust Framework
Monitoring cadence	Periodic audits and manual reviews	Continuous agent logging and real-time dashboards
Scope	Channel- and campaign-specific	System-wide, cross-agent, and signal-level
Primary objective	Prevent infractions	Enable responsible autonomy and adaptive learning
Role of compliance	End-stage reviewer	Co-architect of system logic and escalation protocols
Human intervention	Required for most actions	Reserved for edge cases and ethical gray zones
Attribution	Hard to trace without manual effort	Native explainability in every decision path

Trust doesn't slow the system down.

It makes speed sustainable and defensible.

Trust with Providers

Let's start with the most visible relationship: the one between pharma and healthcare professionals.

In the traditional model, HCPs received:

- Overlapping, repetitive messages from reps and email campaigns.

- Content designed to drive awareness, not relevance.

- Detachment between sales reps and access realities.

- Zero visibility into why they were targeted or what came next.

It created a feeling of noise, **not partnership**.

In the Launchcode model, that experience transforms:

- Engagement becomes **intentional** and **data-aligned.**

- Messaging reflects **clinical and access context.**

- Touchpoints are **fewer**, more personalized, and more coordinated.

- HCP preferences drive delivery format, frequency, and channel mix.

When HCPs feel like the system understands them and respects their time, they engage more fully.

That's trust in action.

Trust with Patients

Patients are more than endpoints in a commercial workflow. They're people navigating therapy decisions, financial strain, emotional uncertainty, and care coordination.

Launchcode's Patient Agent is governed by **ethics-first logic:**

- No nudges without consent.

- No reminders unless clinically relevant.

- No support triggers unless conditions are met.

And messaging is:

- Inclusive.

- Human-centered.

- Language-appropriate.

- Free from judgment.

Because in pharma, **trust equals adherence**.

And trust starts with **how we treat patients when nobody's watching.**

Trust Within the Organization

Systems don't just need external trust. They need **internal trust** to operate at full potential.

Launchcode is designed for cross-functional clarity:

- Sales sees what the brand sees.

- Compliance sees what agents decide.

- Leadership sees the system as not a filtered version of it.

This fosters:

- **Confidence**, not just control.

- **Collaboration**, not just compliance.

- **Action**, not just analysis.

Internal trust isn't a given.

It's earned through **visibility, shared language, and empowerment**.

We often think of trust as something that follows performance. But in AI-powered systems, **trust must precede it**.

It's the foundation that allows performance to scale, experiments to proceed, and innovation to stick.

Launchcode doesn't just earn trust.

It's engineered around it.

Because in the commercial system of the future, trust isn't a side effect of doing things right.

It's the **prerequisite** for doing anything at all.

From Safeguards to Strategic Advantage

Regulation Is Catching Up Fast

If trust is the foundational requirement of AI in pharmaceutical commercialization, regulation is the scaffolding being built around it brick by brick, law by law.

For years, the regulatory environment lagged behind the exponential pace of AI development. Pharma companies operated in the ambiguity between compliance intention and technology execution. But that ambiguity is quickly disappearing.

Global Trends in AI Regulation That Matter to Pharma:

- The FDA is exploring real-time algorithm change protocols and audit trail expectations for AI-enabled medical systems, including commercial ones.

- The EU's General Data Protection Regulation (GDPR) mandates consent-based data use, algorithmic transparency, and explainability in decisions affecting individual patients and HCPs alike.

- HIPAA and the California Consumer Privacy Act (CCPA) are setting stricter limits on data sharing and storage, especially for automated systems processing health data.

- The EU AI Act classifies healthcare-oriented AI as "high-risk," requiring human oversight, robustness documentation, and conformity assessments.

- U.S. legislative proposals now require AI audit trails, bias testing, and real-time override mechanisms.

The implications are clear: If your commercial AI system can't explain its decisions, can't demonstrate consent, and can't show human-in-the-loop governance, it's not just untrusted. It's soon to be unlawful.

Launchcode isn't playing catch-up. It's designed from day one with compliance and ethical readiness as architectural principles not afterthoughts.

Building a Governance Layer That Scales

In Chapter 10, we explored how Launchcode embeds governance within every agent interaction. Here, we go further into how governance becomes a durable, systemic capability.

Four Principles of Scalable Governance:

1. **Distributed Ownership**
   Governance isn't the job of one team. It spans:

   - Brand managers who define strategy boundaries.
   - Compliance officers who codify legal parameters.
   - Data science leaders who monitor drift and fairness.
   - Commercial ops who integrate policies into agent logic.
   - Field and patient support teams who escalate edge-case friction.

2. **Live Monitoring**
   Weekly dashboard reviews flag logic deviations, performance anomalies, or segmentation inequities before they grow systemic. Alerts surface not just incidents but patterns.

3. **Structured Escalation**

When an action breaches a configured threshold:

- The agent pauses execution.
- Human reviewers receive context and rationale.
- Decision paths are traced and reviewed.
- Resolution is logged with a time-stamp and attribution.

4. **Feedback-Informed Learning**

Every override or escalation refines the system:

- Frequent override points suggest rule blind spots.
- Reviewer notes feed next-gen governance logic.
- Drift detection flags where agent behavior diverges from the intended design.

Governance, in this model, is not a wall. It's a set of dynamic, transparent lanes.

Table 15.2: Embedded Governance Capabilities for Launchcode Deployment

Governance Element	Capability
Consent Management	Enforces opt-in status across channels and patient types
Audit Traceability	Logs each agent decision, signal input, and logic path
Threshold Configuration	Sets and tunes safety margins for message types and pacing
Bias Detection	Scans outputs by demographic or geography for disparity
Escalation Workflow	Automates human review when risk or ethics flags are triggered
Explain ability Layer	Generates human-readable logic for agent decisions

These aren't checklists they're capabilities that power responsible scale.

Institutionalizing Ethical Oversight

Ethics in intelligent systems must be more than instinct or intent. They require structure.

Best Practices for Launchcode Ethical Oversight:

1. **Create a Cross-Functional Ethics Review Board**
   Blend perspectives from legal, compliance, patient advocacy, brand strategy, and medical affairs. Review not just violations, but future scenarios and emerging edge cases.

2. **Run "Ethical Foresight" Simulations**
   Before launching a new patient-facing workflow or high-frequency campaign, simulate likely system behavior and surface unintended consequences in advance.

3. **Publish Internal AI Ethics Reports**
   Use quarterly or semiannual summaries to share agent behaviors, escalations, overrides, and ethical findings across functions.

4. **Train for Ethical Judgment**
   Offer team training on how to recognize ethical complexity even when agents don't trigger escalation. Encourage proactive scenario planning and what-if drills.

5. **Promote a Culture of Raising Hands**
   Normalize flagging discomfort even if a process is "technically compliant." Cultural safety creates commercial safety.

Designing for Explainability

Trust requires visibility. But explainability isn't a monolith; it must be designed for multiple audiences:

1. **Field Teams**

   - "Why am I seeing this HCP?"
   - "Why was this message prioritized?"
     Agents respond with natural language summaries, not black box math:
     "This HCP has engaged with recent access messages, but hasn't been visited in 28 days. Your intervention now may lift TRx by 11%."

2. **Brand and Compliance Leads**

   - View dashboards showing which agent rules fired, what logic paths were taken, and whether anything approached a threshold.

3. **Auditors and Regulators**

   - Access a fully traceable decision history inputs, logic flows, overrides, timestamps, and human escalation notes. Exportable, verifiable, defensible.

Explainability is not a luxury. It's how Launchcode earns its license to operate.

Trust as Strategic Advantage

Trust isn't just a safety feature it's a growth strategy.

When trust is embedded:

- Field teams act with clarity and confidence.
- Brand teams test boldly without compliance bottlenecks.

- Patient agents nudge with humanity and timing.

- Regulators see responsibility, not opacity.

- Executive sponsors accelerate investment, not inspection.

Organizations that prioritize explainability, fairness, and alignment aren't just compliant.

They're credible. And credibility earns access, partnership, and competitive advantage.

Final Word

Launchcode doesn't just usher in a new model for commercialization.

It calls for a new model of responsibility.

Because when intelligent agents begin to operate in your name, you need to be confident that they:

- Reflect your values.

- Operate within your guardrails.

- Learn responsibly.

- Surface when they need help.

- And earn trust one interaction at a time.

Designing for trust isn't about compliance checklists or PR messaging.

It's about embedding responsibility into every decision, every message, every escalation, every result.

And when that's in place?

You don't just have a better commercial engine.

You have a system worthy of trust.

Conclusion

The Future Has a Launchcode

We didn't write this book to predict the future.

We wrote it to invite you to build it.

Not with fear. Not with buzzwords. But with purpose, precision, and the kind of clarity that only comes from confronting hard truths.

The old playbook built for blockbuster launches, linear planning, and siloed teams can no longer keep up.

The pace of medicine has outstripped the pace of commercialization. That complexity has become the cost of entry. And that personalization, trust, and adaptability aren't differentiators anymore. Their requirements.

This is a story about reinvention.

About what happens when intelligent systems stop being add-ons and start becoming the infrastructure.

About what's possible when we stop trying to retrofit digital into analog models and start rewriting the operating logic entirely.

About what it means to lead, work, and win in a world where agents learn faster than we can meet.

This Isn't a Vision. It's a Mandate.

We are stepping into an era defined by:

- A $200B patent cliff.

- Complex access barriers and constrained provider time.

- Rare disease fragmentation and personalized therapies.

- AI-native competitors and digitally fluent care teams.

- Global regulatory acceleration and algorithmic scrutiny.

In this landscape, being right slowly is the same as being wrong.

Pharma companies that hesitate won't lose because they didn't care.

They'll lose because they couldn't adapt fast enough.

Those who succeed?

They won't just have better tech. They'll have a system that thinks with them and acts faster than their old teams ever could.

Launchcode isn't your next campaign.

It's your next commercial operating system.

Your Launchcode Is Not a Tool. It's a Philosophy.

It's a belief system disguised as a software stack.

- That speed and safety can coexist.

- That automation doesn't mean dehumanization.

- That compliance can be proactive, not punitive.

- That orchestration beats coordination.

- That commercial systems should serve not just the brand, but the people behind it.

It's a bet on agents that don't just do things but learn from what works. And people who don't just run programs but design better ones every quarter, every signal, every cycle.

It's not just intelligent. It's intentional.

What Happens Next Is Up to You

If you're a **leader**, your job is to sponsor systems that scale curiosity. To move from top-down mandates to signal-driven momentum. And to model the humility that says: the smartest person in the room might now be the system we built together.

If you're a **marketer**, you are no longer the campaign owner. You are the architect of real-time content logic, signal-response trees, and adaptive experience flows. You don't just launch. You learn.

If you're in the **field**, you are the most human node in the system. The one who interprets nuance, resolves ambiguity, and trains the agent through action. You are not being replaced. You are being *amplified*.

If you're in **compliance**, you're not the speed bump. You're the co-pilot. The systems thinker who ensures AI can go fast safely. You're designing trust into every rule, every trigger, every threshold.

If you're in **analytics, ops, or innovation,** you are the connective tissue. You don't just track what worked. You help *decide* what should happen next. You translate noise into a signal. Hypothesis into habit.

This is not just a new model.

It's a new mindset.

This Is the Launch Moment

The agents are real.

The playbooks are live.

The system is ready.

But the real launch code isn't embedded in the software. It's embedded in how you choose to lead.

- Will you wait for the next MLR cycle to act?

- Or will you let the system adapt in real time?

- Will you measure what's easy?

- Or track what actually matters?

- Will you use AI to double down on yesterday's tactics?

- Or to discover tomorrow's orchestration model?

The blueprint is here. The rules have been rewritten. Now it's your turn to activate them.

Final Word

The future of pharmaceutical commercialization isn't faster decks or bigger CRMs.

It's a living system.

- That senses.

- That adapts.

- That learns.

- That earns trust.

- That builds momentum because it's designed to move with the market, not against it.

You don't need another roadmap.

You need to start the engine.

You have the agents.

You have the architecture.

You have the trust framework.

And now, you have the Launchcode.

Time to launch.

www.ingramcontent.com/pod-product-compliance
Lightning Source LLC
Chambersburg PA
CBHW040920210326
41597CB00030B/5139